A Middle School Curriculum

From Rhetoric To Reality

Second Edition

by

James A. Beane

NATIONAL MIDDLE SCHOOL ASSOCIATION

James Beane is a Professor in the National College of Education, National-Louis University and is headquartered in Madison, Wisconsin. A nationally recognized scholar and teacher, Beane's vision, particularly in the areas of curriculum and self-esteem, has been a major influence for educational improvement.

The National Middle School Association is grateful to him for his leadership and is pleased to be able to make this important work on curriculum available to the profession at large.

Appreciation is also expressed to Barbara Brodhagen for her assistance in refining the manuscript and Mary Mitchell for her conscientious work in preparing the copy for printing.

Copyright © 1990, 1993 by National Middle School Association
2600 Corporate Exchange Drive, Suite 370
Columbus, Ohio 43231
Fifth printing April 1998

ISBN: 1-56090-073-3

For my great friend and teacher,

Connie Toepfer

who let me into our profession when no one else would.
I often wonder what he saw, how he knew.

Contents

Foreword

To date, middle level education, despite all its important and needed organizational changes, has seemed to lack a clear vision of what might be, of what attributes our graduates should possess or a philosophically and educationally valid blueprint that would make it possible to put its rhetoric regarding the developmental needs of early adolescents into reality. The need for such a vision has now been met. In this volume, James Beane has thoughtfully and thoroughly reviewed the past, exposed for analysis the separate subject approach, and outlined a proposal for a new general education program that would truly transform the middle level school. This program would reflect the known needs of early adolescents, and it would also deal forthrightly with the equally important needs of contemporary society.

The first edition of this book proved to be something of a catalyst for the middle level curriculum movement that is now well under way. It seemed as if progressive middle level educators were just waiting for such a scholarly assessment, such a sound proposal, and such a clarion call. This second edition will extend the influence of this work of enduring importance. To those who read the first edition, I urge another reading. There is nothing in here but that which warrants a re-reading — and there is here much highly significant new material. In the Preface to the Second Edition, Beane identifies the major new features, features which will make the volume far more functional. In addition, the Preface provides a needed perspective and a more complete context for the chapters that follow.

It is a radical proposal, make no mistake about it. On first reading one may have difficulty conceptualizing it fully. His proposals are beyond the experiences of most everyone. His critique of past and present practices, although fair, may make some readers defensive, for as Francis Bacon reminded us "most people prefer to believe what they prefer to be true." But this treatise deserves and should be given full consideration by every serious middle level professional. The theses presented herein, though they may make educators uncomfortable, need to be understood, analyzed, and discussed. The middle level movement will soon be in danger of losing its steam, of becoming faddish, if it doesn't grapple with the curriculum issues presented here.

We who claim proudly our commitment to kids and to this vibrant movement cannot pass up the opportunity that is ours in the decade of the 90s to seriously reconstitute our schools for young adolescents. This book gives us a vehicle for engaging in dialogue on the critical questions concerning curriculum that we have not confronted adequately.

If the middle school is an idea whose time as come, as we often claim, and the conditions for reform are as ripe as they appear to be, then these cogently presented ideas warrant full consideration. I implore educators to read and ponder what I believe to be a momentous publication.

John H. Lounsbury
Editor, NMSA Publications

Preface to Second Edition

The first edition of this small book appeared in June 1990, not a very long time ago. When I handed over the manuscript to John Lounsbury, the Editor of NMSA Publications, I thought there might be a small audience of interested professors and progressive teachers. I never imagined that raising the middle school curriculum question would strike such a resonant chord among middle level educators in the U.S. and elsewhere. Apparently concern for the curriculum was not buried quite as deeply as I had thought.

This second edition retains most of what was included in the first. But I have also added a good deal. There is a new section on curriculum guidelines that invites people to invent other ways of seeking the broad purposes my own proposal sought to achieve. I have also added material on (1) finding themes, (2) planning with young people, (3) democratic uses of knowledge, (4) getting started with curriculum reform, (5) scheduling around integrated activities, and (6) needed research regarding a new curriculum. In other cases, previous points are elaborated and references added or up-dated. Some material that I now realize was inappropriate or unwise has been dropped.

These revisions did not result from simply sitting in an armchair and thinking. Over the past three years I have had the privilege of visiting with concerned teachers and administrators in a variety of places —

educators who have decided to take action or, happily, to come out from behind closed classroom doors to speak of their many years of experience with integrated, student-centered, democratic curriculum. I see now that legitimating the work of the latter was just as important as encouraging action by the former. I am thinking here of the teacher who has taught in a block-time, integrated core program in Kansas for twenty-six years, of the two in Oregon who told me about their plans late one night when they could just as well have been off enjoying their vacation, of the teams in New Hampshire and Kansas and Arizona and Maine who were carrying on serious curriculum conversations, of the team in Milwaukee, working under adverse conditions to make a curriculum that would make a difference, and of those dazzling teachers in Vermont who have told their stories in *Dancing Through Walls* (Stevenson and Carr, 1993).

Meanwhile, back on the home front in Madison, Wisconsin, I have spent considerable time in seventh and eighth grade classrooms alongside teachers who decided to try an almost literal implementation of the curriculum version I had proposed. To watch these teachers create and carry out an integrative, thematic curriculum, planned from scratch with their students, has been breathtaking to say the least. Sometimes I have felt like a student teacher, at other times I felt thrown back to my own public school teaching days. But having been with these teachers and young adolescents, I surely feel that I know a lot more about curriculum than I did before.

I also learned a great deal as a participant in the Middle Level Curriculum Project, a group of teachers, administrators, state department personnel, and university professors that met several times to discuss possibilities for the middle school curriculum. The collaborative paper we developed (Middle Level Curriculum Project, 1993) emerged from intense and sometimes heated exchange that clarified and sharpened ideas for all of us. Widespread interest in the group's work is certainly a sign that such a curriculum conversation could easily have involved a much larger group.

I am not so naïve as to think that we have yet made a large dent in the curriculum arrangements we seek to change. On the other hand there is clearly room for some optimism: the National Middle School Association's commitment to take on curriculum issues, the special issues of the *Middle School Journal,* the talk about curriculum integration emerging from some subject area associations, the interest shown by some state departments of education and school districts, and so on. Even a few high schools are beginning to ask questions about what is going on at the middle level.

--- **❝❝** ---

The middle level now appears to be the likeliest site for serious conversations about the prospects for fundamental curriculum reform.

This last point is of particular interest. I have been asked many times why I wrote for middle schools when the general theory of integrative curriculum applies to all levels. The answer is really quite simple: middle level educators seem more willing to talk about this topic than others. Perhaps this is because we have become accustomed to thinking about change in our middle schools. Perhaps it is by living with the incredible diversity of early adolescents that we see the need for change more clearly etched. Whatever the reasons, the middle level now appears to be the likeliest site for serious conversations about the prospects for fundamental curriculum reform.

A line of work that matters

Some readers of the first edition apparently had the impression that I invented the curriculum theory it proposed. Perhaps they did not check the dates for some of the references. If they had, they might have correctly seen that the present work is part of a long line that stretches back more than a century. However, the strongest roots, particularly at the middle level, are in the those parts of the progressive movement from the 1930s on that advocated a problem-centered "core" and social reconstruction curriculum. There we can locate calls for such arrangements as a thematic curriculum based upon profound social issues, teacher-student cooperative planning, democratic structures, and a variety of others that we are now trying to revitalize.

Other readers have tied the present work to general trends in the late 1960s and early 1970s. They are right to the extent that we are attempting to be more "child-centered" and are willing to sacrifice some beloved institutional features. However, I suspect that there was something far less coherent about the range of possibilities that were popularized at that time. In some ways we are now much less tempted to throw away the schools than to reconstruct them toward a renewed sense of their most important purposes.

The curriculum version I have proposed adds to earlier work in several ways. first, the concept of self and social meaning, what I elsewhere called "affect" (Beane, 1990), is made the central theme for the entire middle school curriculum rather than simply combining with other interests. Second, what were known as the "problems" and "emerging needs" approaches are merged in the identification of themes at their intersection. Third, the critique of the separate subject approach has a more political edge, especially with regard to culture and power. Fourth, given the progress made in the middle school movement, I have been able to work from some assumptions about climate and organizational structures that are more common in middle level schools now, to say nothing of the rhetoric that has surrounded the movement itself.

Though these additions to earlier efforts should not be construed as a claim for "inventing" a new view of the curriculum, I want to say something here about how I came to make the proposal when and how I did. Early in my career I was fortunate to study with Professor Conrad F. Toepfer at the State University of New York at Buffalo. As most people who have followed the middle school movement know, Toepfer was and is one of its earliest and most forceful advocates. He introduced a group of us to initial work on middle schools and also to important sources from the junior high school movement, several of which can be found in the references for this volume. We professionally "cut our teeth" on that work.

I was particularly enamored with progressive curriculum work like the "problem-centered" and "experience-centered" core curriculum, the work from which my own draws so heavily. In the intervening years though, my own interests also focused on the issue of how schools influence the self-concept/esteem and values of young people. That focus resulted in two volumes with Richard Lipka (Beane and Lipka, 1986, 1987). At about the same time, Toepfer, Samuel Alessi, and I published a book on general curriculum in which we sketched out "classical" curriculum alternatives in a contemporary context (Beane,

Toepfer, and Alessi, 1986). A few years later, I brought these two lines of work together in a volume entitled *Affect in the Curriculum* (Beane, 1990) and extended them in a political and cultural direction by emphasizing the themes of democracy, human dignity, and cultural diversity.

While the last of these was in press, I realized, with the help of Barbara Brodhagen, that all of that previous work might come together and be focused on the middle school curriculum. By that time I was increasingly frustrated by the curriculum talk of the middle school movement which seemed unable to move beyond relatively simple "multi-subject" correlations, the separation of affective topics into isolated "advisory" programs, and the tendency to avoid significant issues like democracy, social problems, and political concerns. Meanwhile, talk about national and state curriculum mandates and testing was accelerating to the detriment (sometimes unnoticed) of the middle school philosophy.

It was also becoming increasingly apparent that middle school educators who had done just about everything recommended to that point were still struggling with some unnamed gap in the movement itself. Among others, Richard Levy of Virginia came right out and named the curriculum. So did the series of "shadow studies" conducted by Lounsbury and others. As if all of this was not enough, the final straw was a statement by a speaker at a middle school conference who said, "it doesn't matter what we teach early adolescents, only how we teach them."

——————— 66 ———————

Early adolescents, their teachers, their parents, and others want a curriculum that is about something of great significance.

Imagine that! Could it be that we attach no importance to the actual content, knowledge, attitudes, predispositions, skills, values, and so on that we bring to early adolescents during this time in their lives? Could it be that early adolescents themselves don't care either? Could it be that there is nothing of compelling value beyond climate and process that middle schools ought to be about? Could it be that curriculum is nothing more than an afterthought in our middle schools? I hardly think so! And I think that early adolescents, their teachers, their parents, and others want a curriculum that is about something of great significance.

In the epilogue of the first edition, left intact for this one, I named the larger purpose for the current curriculum work: "It is to open the hearts and minds of young people to the possibilities for a more just and humane world — a world in which human dignity, the democratic way of life, and the prizing of diversity are more widely shared and experienced." Certainly that says something about how we teach. But it also says something about what we teach. And I think that matters.

A word about language

Disenchantment with the "traditional" curriculum has led educators and others to begin moving away from the strict subject-centered approach. Many now talk about replacing subjects as organizing centers with "themes." But this does not tell us what those themes or their sources might be. Some speak of finding themes from the existing curriculum that will encourage correlation across two or more subjects — what I refer to as *a multidisciplinary* approach. Others speak of finding themes in social problems or in the issues facing young people in relation to development. In either case, some still use a multidisciplinary planning approach ("What can each subject area contribute?"), while others are willing to ignore subject area lines and instead draw from any subject area without regard for boundaries or identification, while focusing on the problem or issue at hand. This is what I would call *curriculum integration,* although that term has also been used with regard to "integrating" things like thinking, health, and writing across the subjects.

A few teachers (not enough, I think) are interested in planning the curriculum with young people in terms of questions and concerns they have about themselves and their world. In this case knowledge and skill are integrated naturally and by the young people themselves as they carry out their work. Experiences are integrated into present schemes of meaning and new ones are constructed. This I would call an *integrative curriculum* since the purpose is to help young people integrate their experiences on their own terms rather than those of adults.

In the current talk about curriculum these terms are used rather loosely. "Thematic" is used to cover everything but really means nothing without saying what the themes are about. "Integration" is often used to refer to "multi-disciplinary" experiences, which sidesteps the issue of whether the latter are more than mere tinkering with the separate subject approach. In this sense "multi-disciplinary" is not used enough since it is the most widely used of the approaches that are not strictly subject centered. "Integrative" has been less commonly used than any and though it is gaining prominence, it too is being used to cover less than it really means. And worst of all, "interdisciplinary" has come to mean little more than whatever a multi-subject team of teachers wants to do.

In the first edition of this book I simply called my proposal a "new" curriculum. I have tried in some of my other writing and lectures to tie that "new" curriculum to those terms just discussed, perhaps in some ways contributing to the language confusion. In preparing this present version, therefore, I have been faced with the question of now naming my proposed curriculum. Frankly I wish I could call it "core" as that term was properly used in earlier days or even "integration" or "integrative," the more recent terms. But each of these has been appropriated to mean so many things and I am not inclined to invent a new term that would likely be appropriated as well.

To avoid all of this I have decided to again call it a "new" curriculum. Besides, it is "new" given what we have had for too long. Some people have called it "Beane's curriculum" but they are wrong about that, especially in the historical sense. Imagine if they called it "the middle school curriculum" implying thereby that any other would be inappropriate and therefore not eligible to be attached to the middle school. But if "new" is not enough and if "the middle school curriculum" is too dangerous, I wish people would call it "a curriculum for early adolescents." After all, that is what I meant it to be.

Prologue

The purpose of this small volume is to open up the middle school curriculum question. Put simply, that question is this: What ought to be *the* curriculum of the middle school. By italicizing the word "the" in this question I mean to be clear that I am not asking about various parts of the typical middle school program, like academic or "special" subjects, but rather about the broad and underlying conception of the whole curriculum at this level.

Put this way, the middle school curriculum question is an intriguing one. Over the past three decades efforts to improve schooling at the middle level have made considerable progress. However these efforts have mainly addressed better understanding of early adolescents and the organizational structures of the middle school. To a lesser degree, and with less success, they have sometimes spoken to the correlation of subject areas through "interdisciplinary" instruction and the modification of teaching methods to accommodate the characteristics of "kids." Meanwhile, the broader "curriculum question" has received far less attention. Yet it is hard to imagine an authentic school improvement project at any level that does not involve rethinking the curriculum since the curriculum is a central and crucial factor in the life of a school. Thus the curriculum question has been an "absent presence" in the middle school movement.

1

My own sense of this dilemma is that entering such territory is very risky business. For example, many middle level educators have deep loyalties to particular subject areas and subject matter and their professional self-concepts are partially defined by them: teachers are not just "teachers;" they are "English teachers," "music teachers," "math teachers," and so on. Moreover, the education field as a whole is largely organized around these subject distinctions, including the language it uses to describe its work.

I want to suggest that the work on middle school organization and teaching methods has succeeded partly, and perhaps mostly, because it has focused on better ways of transmitting the usual subject matter without questioning that subject matter or the subject area curriculum organization that surrounds it. The difficulty often experienced in promoting even modest subject correlations through interdisciplinary teams certainly supports this criticism as does, for example, the hot debate over heterogeneous grouping, an arrangement that many see as interfering with academic achievement. Taken this way, the "absent presence" of the broader curriculum question could partly be accounted for by fear that explicitly asking it might just cause a rift in what has mostly been a gentle and friendly reform movement at the middle level.

Yet I do not see how we can continue to progress in that reform work without taking on this question. Middle school advocates have claimed from the beginning that their primary concern is with the characteristics of early adolescence. If those characteristics are extended into a discussion of the curriculum, it becomes apparent that the persistent organization around a collection of academic and "special" courses, with emphasis on the former, is not a developmentally appropriate nor genuinely responsive approach to the curriculum. Surely there must be a different and better answer to the curriculum question, an answer that more closely matches the curriculum with ongoing rhetoric about middle schools.

Chapter 1 of this volume opens up the middle school curriculum question by looking back at the beginning of the so-called "middle school movement" to see where the curriculum fits in, as well as the pressures that are exerted on the curriculum both inside and outside the school. Chapter 2 involves a look at how the curriculum question has been addressed in middle school theory and practice over the past thirty years. Here some of the major texts of that period are reviewed as well as what goes on in middle school in the name of "curriculum."

Chapter 3 presents an admittedly unkind critique of the separate subject, academic-centered approach to the curriculum. If we are going to take on the curriculum question in a genuine way, then we must recognize how that approach has so seriously failed the middle schools and so frequently helped to create a deadening effect on teaching and learning. Chapter 4 presents a theory of what I think the middle school curriculum ought to be and how it ought to be organized. The major idea behind this approach is that the middle school ought to be a "general education" school whose curriculum is formed around the emerging and common developmental concerns of early adolescents and the widely shared issues that face people in the larger world, regardless of the individual paths their lives take. It is in the intersection of these personal and social concerns that I will propose we find the themes around which the curriculum ought to be organized.

Chapter 5 will involve a look at some of the tasks that lie ahead if we are to carry out curriculum reform. Clearly we will need some serious discussion of the middle school curriculum before taking specific action, but just as clearly we will have to be willing to rethink many policies and procedures if the curriculum itself takes on a new form. In Chapter 6 I will summarize the case I have made and its implications for the future of middle level schools.

I am acutely aware that when we speak of "curriculum," we ought to mean the totality of learning experiences in the school and that the processes we use and the institutional features of the school constitute a part of that meaning. However, in this proposal I will speak to the planned curriculum and particularly its content. Much has already been said about the "hidden curriculum" of the middle school in the work on climate and structural organization. How my proposal fits with that work is partly shown in Chapter 5 and should otherwise be implicitly clear to anyone who has followed the middle school movement over the past few decades.

Those of us who have been involved in the middle school movement in the United States should also understand that the dilemma I am addressing here is not unique to this country. Indeed, it is one that has marked such work in other countries as seen, for example, in comparing proposals by John Burrows (1978) and Andy Hargreaves (1986) regarding middle schools in England and in the multinational descriptions presented in an issue of the *Middle School Journal* (September, 1989) devoted to that purpose.

Finally, I hope that those who have been involved in the middle school movement will take my critique of their work in good spirit. Like so many others, I recognize that the progress toward reform has been remarkable in many middle schools. Indeed, it is often at the middle level, more than at others, that we can look today for examples of school practices that clearly lean toward the best interests of young people. Moreover, it would be foolish not to recognize the significant contributions made by middle level theorists to that progress. In many ways, the congruence between theory and practice is closer at this level than at any other. Yet I also firmly believe that the possibility for extending this success story cannot be realized apart from the central curriculum question that has been avoided for too long.

In developing the ideas in this work I called upon several friends for help. They included Michael Apple, Ken Bergstrom, Barbara Brodhagen, Peggy Burke, Gail Burnaford, Ray Johnson, David Chawszczewski, Jim Ladwig, Richard Levy, John Lounsbury, Lee McDonough, Ed Mikel, Allison Mudrick, Joyce Shanks, and Gordon Vars. The infamous Friday Group at the University of Wisconsin was especially helpful in thinking about curriculum guidelines and the democratic uses of knowledge. Needless to say all of these people did not agree with my view of the way things ought to be, but their questions, comments, and suggestions forced me to clarify many issues and to think more deeply about the curriculum. And so do the continuing conversations with colleagues in the Department of Interdisciplinary Studies at National-Louis University, especially Mary Manke. I take full responsibility for what is written here, but I hope they will understand how much their assistance was appreciated. Finally, I want to thank the teachers and administrators at Marquette Middle School in Madison, Wisconsin for letting me into their school and allowing me to be a colleague.

1.

The Middle School Curriculum Question

E fforts to reform middle level education have made considerable progress in the thirty years of the middle school movement, particularly with regard to developing more widespread awareness of the characteristics of early adolescence and reorganizing institutional features, such as school climate. Important as these are, the movement has largely come to be seen as limited to them. Indeed, as more and more school districts become involved in middle level reorganization, the most pressing questions seem to revolve around an effort to replicate what has become the standard list of middle school features — interdisciplinary team organization, block scheduling, advisory programs, student activities, and so on. Largely obscured in this search for improved middle level education has been what is probably the most critical question in this or any other kind of authentic school reform:

What should be the curriculum of the middle school ?

Joan Lipsitz (1984, p. 188) put this succinctly in her classic work, *Successful Schools for Young Adolescents:* "translating philosophy into curriculum is the most difficult feat for schools to accomplish...the translation to climate and organizational structure appears to be much easier..." Five years later, Edward Brazee (1989) echoed this frustration in saying that, "curriculum development has not kept pace with overall

5

middle level program development, in spite of the many successes of middle level education in the past twenty-five years."

This condition was foreshadowed when in comparing the 1977 shadow study of the eighth grade with the 1962 shadow study of the seventh grade, the authors commented: "The major differences between 1962 and 1977 may be in climate rather than curriculum, in the atmosphere more than the course of study." (Lounsbury, Marani & Compton, 1977, p. 65)

Again in the 1989 shadow study of the eighth grade this generalization was reconfirmed. The data led the authors to conclude:

> Progress in climate is more apparent than progress in curriculum. Positive attitudes toward students, genuine concern for them and their developmental needs is evident, but the curriculum of content remains largely unchanged, even in many teamed situations. Schools have instituted recognition programs, developed fun activities like a dress-up day, organized interdisciplinary teams, established special classes or arrangements for students with unusual needs — all to the good — but the curriculum of content, the bread and butter of the school program, still is not reflective of what is known about the nature and needs of early adolescents. (Lounsbury and Clark, 1990, p. 133)

The importance of the fundamental but bypassed "curriculum question" cannot be overestimated since it opens the way to several key issues that supposedly guide the middle school movement but are only partially addressed by organizational reform. For example, if early adolescence is a distinct stage in human development and if the middle school is to be based on the characteristics of that stage, then presumably the curriculum would be designed along developmentally appropriate lines and would thus look different from that at other levels. If "reform" means that the relationship between schools, including teachers, and early adolescents are to be reconstructed, then the curriculum, as one of the powerful mediating forces in that relationship, would presumably be changed.

Quite likely many inside the middle school movement perceive that curriculum change has taken place. They might, for instance, point to different instructional procedures, interdisciplinary teaming, improved guidance through advisory programs, efforts to expand school-sponsored activities, and the like. However, asking "how to teach" is not the same as asking "what to teach." Nor is the matter of simply adding onto existing programs necessarily the appropriate response to new curriculum expectations. I do not want to separate "curriculum" and instruction here or to suggest that broadening conceptions of what the school ought to offer is not a curriculum issue. Rather I want to recognize that these are only part of a more comprehensive question about curriculum.

―――――――――――― 〝 ――――――――――――

The movement has succeeded partly because it has not taken on substantive change that would touch deep subject matter loyalties.

In opening up the question about what ought to be the middle school curriculum, we face what is sure to be a more perilous journey than the one the movement has taken to date. That movement has, no doubt, succeeded to the extent it has partly because it has not been attached to any larger social or political reform efforts that might bring it into conflict with dominant, powerful interests and partly because it has not taken on substantive curriculum change that would touch the deep subject matter loyalties held by educators both inside and outside middle schools.

To understand how this could have happened, we must return to the initial days of the movement and realize how it was launched. In the late 1950s and early 1960s, elementary schools faced severe overcrowding as the "baby boom" moved through the schools. Relieving this pressure might have been accomplished in several ways, not the least of which would have meant building new elementary schools. However, the prohibitive cost of such an undertaking was hardly attractive. On the other hand, it was also possible to move some of the children out of the overcrowded schools if a place could be found for them.

Here, then, was a more acceptable plan: if an addition was built onto the high school or a new high school or middle school constructed, then ninth graders could be moved to the high school and fifth and/or sixth graders moved to a middle level school. Certainly, this option would be more acceptable to the taxpayers who would have to foot the bill. At the same time, the matter of moving some children out of the elementary school offered an important possibility in metropolitan areas. The neighborhood elementary school had long been the bastion of *de facto* racial segregation. Reorganizing grade levels in the middle meant that those elementary schools would contain fewer years in the school sequence and children would thus move out of them sooner and into a more integrated middle level school.

Meanwhile, the junior high school organization had come under serious criticism from a quite different direction. For one thing, many commentators raised persistent doubts that what had become simply a junior version of the high school was appropriately serving the characteristics of early adolescents as it had been intended to do. For another, research by J.M. Tanner (1962) and others had suggested that the decreasing age for achieving puberty ought to redefine the ages normally associated with early adolescence; that is, instead of ages 12 to 14, ages 10 or 11 to 13 now appeared more accurate from a physiological perspective. Primarily in light of these two factors a number of educators began to speak of a new configuration of grades five or six through eight for the middle level and simultaneously of a renewed spirit of experimentation within that level.

It is in the convergence of these two strands, overcrowding and desegregation on the one hand and research about early adolescence and dissatisfaction with the junior high school on the other, that we can begin to see the emergence of what would become the middle school movement. During the 1960s books and journal articles about "middle schools," some of which will be reviewed in Chapter 2, began to appear and professional organizations, such as the Association for Supervision and Curriculum Development, began to take an interest in early adolescents and their schools. From the standpoint of school practice, it must have been somewhat confounding to principals and teachers who attended "middle school" sessions at conferences expecting to hear about grade level reorganization to hear instead that changing grade levels was only a part of the story being told.

As the 1970s unfolded this trend continued with a proliferation of workshops and institutes about middle schools, the founding of the National Middle School Association, the Center for Early Adolescence in North Carolina, the National Middle School Resource Center in Indiana, and several state and regional middle school associations. With the increasing numbers of publications about middle schools, the growing body of research about early adolescence, and the organization of professional educators interested in the middle level, observers of the scene could see all of the signs of a "movement." And certainly there was no decrease in the level of activity regarding middle schools in the 1980s. Indeed, that decade culminated with the wide dissemination of *Turning Points: Preparing American Youth for the 21st Century* (Carnegie Council on Adolescent Development, 1989), a publication that turned the spotlight onto the middle level.

Early literature about the new middle schools suggests that several themes guided the beginnings of the movement and hints at how curriculum considerations fit into that scene. One persistent and very proper theme was developing understanding about and sensitivity to the characteristics of early adolescents — new information about the stage was appearing at an impressive rate. A second theme was elevation of the middle school out of the second-class status the junior high had come to hold in school organization. A third was to differentiate the junior high school from the high school, a task that historical efforts had failed to accomplish. A fourth theme centered around structural change including the organization of some teachers into interdisciplinary teams, the inclusion of activities (or interest-centered) programs, and the use of block scheduling.

And what of the curriculum? Unlike the other themes, this one had a somewhat confusing and contentious place in middle school talk. Theorists who served as leaders in those early days were largely those who continued from the junior high school movement: William Alexander, Conrad Toepfer, John Lounsbury, Gordon Vars, Gertrude Noar, Mauritz Johnson, William Gruhn, and others. As such, they brought to the new middle school movement the same disagreements and range of ideas about an appropriate middle school curriculum that were the source of debate in the junior high school movement. While some advocated use of a "core" program organized around emerging adolescent characteristics and social problems, others favored only organizational changes at the middle level with continuation of a subject centered, largely academic curriculum. With all of the "change" talk at the middle level, it was undoubtedly very reassuring for local educators to hear a key "middle school" figure remark, "such grade reorganization does not necessarily involve any change in the instructional program...the departmentalized schedule and the same program of activities may carry over into the new school..." (Alexander, 1966, p. 31).

It is also important to remember that the 1960s saw a reemphasis on the subject area curriculum following the launching of Sputnik. For many junior high schools, that turn of events had meant that block-time, problem-centered core programs died the day Sputnik went up. Much of the general curriculum rhetoric of the decade that followed was, of course, basically the same as that heard in the 1980s from classical humanists and social efficiency advocates who claimed their position as a response to the "Japanese economic threat," the contemporary version of the "Russian space threat."

In retrospect, we may now see that the curriculum question was a problematic one from the very beginning of the middle school movement. Moreover, we can begin to sense how it has been that the themes of understanding early adolescents and creating structural changes in the school, important as they may be, have obscured the critical curriculum question. And we can fairly imagine how those themes have given those who want to avoid the curriculum question a safe place to hide in the middle level "reform" movement. Yet I do not want to imply that confronting this question, let alone responding to it, presents an easy or comfortable situation. Quite to the contrary, the myriad of pressures on the middle school curriculum make this a very difficult one.

Pressures on the middle school curriculum

The planned curriculum of the middle school, like that of any other level, is subject to and created by a number of forces. In the rhetoric of most middle school theory, the primary force is the *characteristics of early adolescence*. As we have seen, understanding of and sensitivity to these characteristics has been a continuing theme from the early days of the middle school movement. Indeed, with the grade level argument generally put to rest, we might now define the middle school as one that may take diverse forms in particular locations, but is consistent in being developmentally appropriate to early adolescence. Presumably, this view would apply to the curriculum of the middle school as well as other features.

In reality, of course, that is only one of several forces that loom at least as large in middle schools. Another is the *curriculum mandates* that are handed down to schools through federal and state legislation, state board policies, as well as district regulations, including often specific accompanying standardized tests. Most recently this pressure may be found in the general trend toward increased centralization of curriculum and other policy decisions and the loss of local control in schools. Nowhere is this pressure more vividly portrayed than in the flood of state mandates following the release of *A Nation at Risk* in 1983 (National Commission on Excellence in Education).

Ostensibly directed toward high schools, that report and many of the subsequent state mandates nevertheless seriously affected the middle school inasmuch as the proposed increases in high school graduation meant that advanced placement and introductory high school courses were pushed into the middle schools. As a result, many middle school educators saw important pieces of their programs, such as multidisciplinary units, block schedules, and heterogeneous grouping, chipped away.

Given the fact that almost all of the talk about middle school reform was carried out only among middle level educators, it is possible that this situation might not have bothered the authors of that Commission report or the mandates since they probably knew little about what had been happening at the middle level. On the other hand, the appearance of "academic rigor" in this report was undoubtedly welcomed by many middle level educators who felt that the movement was too "permissive" in its emphasis on sensitivity to early adolescent characteristics. Of course as the 1990s unfold, all of this may seem "small pickings" compared to the ominous possibility of a national testing/curriculum system largely constructed out of the same misguided intentions.

This pressure is extended, and the next one reinforced, by the media and academicians who prey on the fears of parents by insisting that nothing less than more and earlier academic pressure will put their children on the path to college and career success. As a result, almost any talk about curriculum change is liable to be lumped in with trading state secrets and other seditious acts.

A third pressure is the *expectations of parents and the society as a whole* about the education of their children. Most adults experienced middle level education within the "junior version of the high school" model and no doubt expect the same for succeeding generations of early adolescents. On the other hand, the adult society also interprets youth "needs" in light of contemporary social problems at any historical moment. In this sense, expectations beyond the subject program of the school are formed and become ones to which the schools are expected to respond (although they may not be directly asked to do so). These expectations include development of "desired" work skills and attitudes, prevention of substance abuse, pregnancy, crime, and so on.

---------------------- **66** ----------------------

The dominant version of the middle school has had two major features, the separate subject approach and separate programs for different purposes.

A fourth pressure is the *structures of tradition* that arise out of the historic curriculum orientation of the middle level school. As we have already seen, that orientation has been contested by various alternatives but the dominant version of the middle school has had two major features. One of these is the use of a separate subject approach. The other is the definition of separate programs for different purposes such as academics, "exploration," guidance, and interest-centered activities, with the academic portion seen as the most important. One cannot overestimate the power of these structures of tradition or the very deep loyalties many middle school educators have to them. It is quite likely that many simply cannot conceive of any other way of organizing the curriculum let alone any other way of doing so.

A fifth pressure, and one related to that just described, is the *interests of subject area specialists at all levels* who seek to define what is appropriate for their own area. Here we may place the interests of professional subject area associations, university academics, state department and district curriculum officials, and subject teachers within middle schools as they engage in continuing discussions about what ought to be taught and in what way. At the same time, one cannot help but notice that such discussions also have the side effect of limiting curriculum thinking to the subject approach and thus marginalizing any other form.

A sixth pressure is *theories and proposals about middle level reform itself.* While several of these will be taken up in Chapter 2, they generally fall into two positions. One focuses on finding ways of making traditional subject areas more agreeable to early adolescents, mainly through use of improved instructional techniques such as cooperative learning and multidisciplinary correlations. The other position advocates some type of curriculum reform such as block-time "core" programs. As we will see, the former is clearly the more popular.

A seventh pressure is *concerns and interests of local educators* within and outside the middle schools. While I have already commented on the general trend toward centralization of curriculum planning, it is still the case that when the classroom door closes, teachers have a certain degree of control over the curriculum in terms of what they emphasize or de-emphasize. This is particularly true in states where mandates leave substantial room for local interpretation. Moreover, teachers at the high school level expect that certain things will be learned in the middle school and frequently make their wishes known with vocal force. Such hand-me-down expectations (and accompanying criticism) form what is almost a cliché in education and one that is not always strongly resisted.

Finally, though very important, pressure is brought to bear on the middle school curriculum by the *expectations of particular early adolescents in local schools.* As teachers and other adults seek to implement the planned curriculum, early adolescents respond in varying ways from enthusiastic engagement to outright resistance (Apple, 1982). Within the context of such interactions, the curriculum itself is frequently modified to reduce resistance or, occasionally, to digress on paths of student interest. While external curriculum officials often fail to comprehend this reality, it is well known to those who work within the school.   And the everyday life of the curriculum as teachers experience it sometimes inclines them to believe that this is the most powerful pressure of all.

The simultaneous presence of these forces creates a problematic situation for the middle school curriculum inasmuch as there are very real conflicts among them. For example, the interests of adults and those of early adolescents are notoriously different as are the perceptions of important issues held by state officials from those of local educators. Likewise, advocates of middle level reform are continually troubled by the persistent presence of those who cling to the "junior high school" version of middle level education. Such conflict is exacerbated by the fact that those loyal to any particular force or pressure take their views very seriously and are not necessarily ignorant of other alternatives, as much as advocates of those alternatives might insist they are.   The configuration of these various forces and pressures form a not-so-peaceful coexistence among competing interests and, as a result, help to create contradictions and tensions in the everyday curriculum of the middle schools and in the lives of the adults and young people who are a part of them.

Deciding what *ought* to be the basis for the middle school curriculum involves making choices from the array of possible interpretations about what is important to learn. To avoid choosing and thus to try to include all interpretations may appear to be politically wise, but such action can only lead to a momentary and false equilibrium in the middle school. If all positions appear in the school to be equally legitimate while their advocates continue to think otherwise, tensions and contradictions will surely continue and a "showdown" is inevitable.

Likewise, if the middle school simply drifts with whatever position is politically popular, then the curriculum will be continually subjected to the whims and fancies of whoever speaks loudest at any given moment. This can hardly be a defensible version of the middle school curriculum, particularly since those whims and fancies are often at odds with the best interests of early adolescents — interests that the middle school movement ostensibly cherishes.

The present state of the middle school curriculum represents something of a failure of nerve in this regard. That is, the planned curriculum of a growing number of middle schools consists of a collection of specific programs intended to meet all expectations, interdisciplinary teams to create subject area correlations but still based on subject identities, "exploratory" courses to cover technical and aesthetic concerns (and to provide planning time for "academic teachers"), advisory programs to address personal-social development, activities programs to serve individual interests, and so on. While such a plan helps to maintain a kind of equilibrium among competing interests, it also creates a fragmented collection of curriculum pieces without any coherent or broadly unifying theme.

_____ **‘‘** _____

The middle school curriculum is not really a "curriculum" in the sense of having some clearly identifying purpose or theme.

In other words, the middle school curriculum is not really a "curriculum" in the sense of having some clearly identifying purpose or theme that grows out of a widely held definition of what middle level education ought to be about. In this sense it is what it has been from the beginning of the middle school movement and, for that matter, what it had become in the junior high school movement. But the latter is less open to criticism since it never quite made the claims for "reform" that the advocates of the middle school movement have. Yet those advocates must know that the movement to date has only taken us so far toward the realization of what is rhetorically called a middle school. And the movement is bound to stagnate unless it makes new progress. The most obvious direction is to finally take on the middle school curriculum

Creating guidelines for a middle school curriculum

Middle schools included, asking what the curriculum of any school ought to be is a very tricky proposition. Beleaguered by the exigencies of school life and seeking advice from presumed "experts," educators often desire an answer in the form of some document or package that is, for them, "a" curriculum. And certainly there are many outside the school who can't wait to deliver an answer in exactly that way. Remember, for example, the "teacher-proof" curriculum packages of the 1960s and the current "programs" for self-esteem or character education as well as the subject-centered ones that are so frequently advertised in professional journals.

In responding to this version of curriculum thinking. I want to speak very bluntly: there is no such "curriculum." Persons outside of the school, no matter what their credentials, cannot possibly account for all of the diverse aspects of local places that loom so large in the prospects for creating a valuable curriculum. Worse yet, a "curriculum" developed apart from the teachers and young people who must live it is grossly undemocratic in the ways it deprives them of their right to have a say in their own lives and to learn and apply the skills and understandings associated with making important decisions. In the area of curriculum planning and development, we ought to have learned this lesson by now: distance breeds contempt.

_____   **"**   _____

A curriculum developed apart from the teachers and young people who must live it is grossly undemocratic.

So it is that in answering the middle school curriculum question there is no recipe, no detailed map — nor should we want one. What we need instead are serious conversations in local schools aimed at opening up possibilities for teachers and young people to create a curriculum that is significant for and makes sense in their own lives. While there is no precise map, I believe that there is a compass to guide our thinking. That is, we can imagine what those curriculum conversations might be about.

Imagine a conversation that follows a kind of parallel structure. Along one line are ideas about what we want for our young people as well as the characteristics or qualities that a responsive curriculum might have. Along the other line are the varieties of practical curriculum activities or forms. Our conversations, then, are about the interactions between these two lines of thinking: how can what we want be brought to life in practical situations and how do those situations inform continued thinking about what we want?

Contrary to what many of us learned in school, quantum physicists now tell us that parallel lines do meet (somewhere out there). In the sense of the parallel structure I am suggesting, it is at that (or those) point(s) stories emerge which offer practical responses to the curriculum question. Again, though, those stories cannot tell others exactly what to do since each story is created out of local conditions. On the other hand, such stories may well serve to inspire people who want to do something about the curriculum but have a hard time imagining new possibilities. They cannot "do" the same story, but perhaps they can do something like it and thus create their own stories and enlighten their own conversations.

Guidelines for a middle school curriculum

Although recognizing the necessity of local planning, I now want to sketch out several qualities that I believe should be brought to life in the middle school curriculum. As such they serve as guidelines for thought and deliberation; they present what I believe is "desirable" regardless of the practical obstacles that may interfere with their realization. Later I will make a proposal for a "curriculum" that does bring them to life. But mine is only one voice. Surely there are others who might take the same guidelines and create a quite different version of practice. In fact, curriculum practices created out of these guidelines may well be as many as there are classrooms and schools. My proposal is meant to illustrate a possibility; it is not meant to be "the" version everyone must do. This is what the conversation is about. And it should also be about the guidelines themselves: Are they desirable? What do they mean? Are they enough? Are they clear?

1. The middle school curriculum should focus on general education.

Such a curriculum would be concerned with common learnings for all rather than learnings that are differentiated by special interests or student labels. The kind of curriculum differentiation that has characterized so many middle level schools (and programs) begins the unfortunate process of "sorting and selecting" young people, a process that is detrimental to all, but particularly harsh for those who are "non-privileged." Moreover, neither early adolescents nor the adults who work with them are in a position to predict what paths individual lives may follow in the future.

Specialization tends to overemphasize individualism and fracture the sense of common purpose that often emerges in early adolescence. This does not mean that the curriculum should ignore the interests of individuals, but rather that the primary focus should be on a widely shared experience of the kind that we would want all early adolescents to have together regardless of who they are or what they may do in the future.

2. The central purpose of the middle school curriculum should be helping early adolescents explore self and social meanings at this time in their lives.

The middle school is not a "farm system" for the high school, the university, or the interests of business and industry nor is it simply another distribution point for "high-culture capital." Certainly there are many pressures on the curriculum that cannot be ignored, including legislated mandates, subject area interests, and parental expectations. But these must be taken as secondary to the more compelling concerns of what is going on in and around the present lives of early adolescents.

3. The middle school curriculum should respect the dignity of early adolescents.

Most early adolescents as well as adults who care deeply about them are tired of hearing these young people characterized by demeaning, insensitive metaphors like "hormones with feet," "brain-dead," and "range of the strange." Worse yet, even the presumably sensitive litany of "characteristics of early adolescence," typically ignores such issues as culture and tends to freeze early adolescents within that socially constructed "stage" as if there is nothing more to their lives (Brazee and Dibiase, 1992).

Those who really listen to early adolescents know that at both personal and social levels many are concerned about the environment, prejudice, injustice, poverty, hunger, war, politics, violence and the threat these issues pose to the future of our world. Clearly these are not the superficial concerns one would expect to hear from "hormones with feet." To ignore or trivialize these concerns by pressing on with the usual curriculum fare or repackaging it in "cute" activities degrades the dignity of early adolescents and helps block their access to critical knowledge and skill (Arnold, 1980).

4. The middle school curriculum should be firmly grounded in democracy.

We ostensibly live in a democratic society and there are no reasonable grounds that suggest why the democratic way of life should not be extended to early adolescents or into their schools. The democracy I mean, though is not simply a matter of individuals selecting alternatives from a menu of limited choices nor the pseudo-democratic "engineering of consent" around predetermined possibilities. In short, it is not simply whatever someone wants to do or whatever someone can get them to do. Rather I mean that the curriculum ought to be democratically conceived through collaborative planning with involvement of early adolescents — they should have a say and their say should count for something. The voices of teachers are not meant to be silent here but neither are they the persistently dominating source of power and authority over young people. The key concept is "collaboration," the building of communities in which the interests of all people, adults and the young, are sources of curriculum concern.

Furthermore, in a democratic curriculum, information or "facts" brought into the classroom should be open to critical analysis rather than presented for passive assimilation. After all, knowledge is socially constructed by people; it does not spring forth from some mysterious source. Critical questions — "Who said this? Why did they say it? Why should we believe it?" — should permeate classroom life. And out of these kinds of questions, early adolescents ought to be invited to construct their own meanings as active participants in the democratic way of life. Middle school advocates have long spoken of the search for value and moral reasons among early adolescents, a "characteristic" that cries out for a democratic curriculum.

5. The middle school curriculum should honor diversity.

While the notion of general education calls for "common learnings," early adolescents are a diverse group. The curriculum ought to honor this diversity with respect to both content and meanings that are constructed in relation to culture. Considerable progress is being made with respect to inclusion of resources and viewpoints that are multicultural. The middle school curriculum, like others, should seek to expand this progress. So too should it respect diversity of learning styles and other personal factors. And among the cultures and styles that we seek to recognize, we should not forget those that are produced by young people themselves, both individually and collectively.

But honoring diversity means more than just adding a story or two, a display case for ethnic artifacts, or celebrating minority achievements for a day or month. We live in a culturally diverse world. The lives, histories, and contributions of diverse people are not different stories of the human community. Rather they are unique parts of the same story. A curriculum that honors diversity prizes differences but integrates those into a unified understanding of our interdependence. Such a curriculum offers a glimpse of a transformed human community in which both unity and diversity have a secure place.

6. The middle school curriculum should be of great personal and social significance.

Those who work at the middle level enter into the lives of early adolescents for a relatively brief period of time. That time ought to be spent wisely. The curriculum in these years ought to center on powerful themes that enlighten the search for self and social meaning. Many adults have favorite units and activities — the ones on "ancient Egypt" or "baseball" — that they love to do each year. These units may often appeal to young people, especially if they involve fun or exciting activities. However, even with evidence of teacher and student enthusiasm we must still ask whether the school time we have with early adolescents should be spent on topics having questionable personal and social significance.

7. The middle school curriculum should be lifelike and lively.

Significant learning in real life involves having experiences which are integrated into our present scheme of meanings about ourselves and our world so that those meanings are refined, extended, and expanded. Moreover, when confronted with problems or puzzling situations, we typically call forth whatever knowledge and skill we have to resolve them, and if the problem is significant enough, we seek pertinent knowledge and skill we do not already have. Thus a life-like curriculum would call our attention to problems, draw upon relevant, integrated knowledge and skill, and take us further toward self and social meaning.

It is also important to note here that the idea of having all the knowledge and skills necessary to resolve significant problems or situations is impossible. In the real lives unfolding before our very eyes, knowledge is expanding at such a dazzling rate that we simply cannot keep up with it all. A real life curriculum, then, must emphasize ways of gaining access to knowledge and skills as the need for them arises. In this sense, the curriculum ought to be one in which we are all learners regardless of our age or position in the school.

Beyond this, though, the middle school curriculum ought to be lively. Focusing on the serious matter of self and social meaning should not mean reducing activity to "talking heads." Instead, the curriculum should be full of wonder and curiosity. Opportunities should abound for making, doing, and creating things through multiple and creative forms of expression. While helping early adolescents to clarify and refine questions and concerns, we should avoid discouraging those that may seem odd or far-fetched to adults but which are nonetheless a source of curiosity for the restless minds of youth. And when questions or concerns point to injustice in the larger world, we must set aside our own fear of controversy and make way for young people to strengthen their own courage by speaking out and taking action.

8. The middle school curriculum should enhance knowledge and skills for all young people.

Important knowledge and skills are necessary for extending self and social meaning. Thus the curriculum must promote such knowledge and skills lest it work against the best interests of young people. On the other hand, if the curriculum is life-like, knowledge and skills would enter in insofar as they support self and social meaning. This condition means that we will likely be dealing with some knowledge and skills that have not surfaced in the past while deleting some that have, but which are trivial or overly abstract.

However, we must be very careful in making decisions about knowledge and skill. Historically, some so-called "progressive" or "child-centered" curriculum plans have given short shrift to knowledge and skills which are needed for access to various places or positions in our society. While "privileged" young people may acquire these anyway, such plans, exciting as they may be, may backfire on those who are "non-privileged" and whose cultures and environments may not automatically pass on this kind of cultural capital. Furthermore, "official" knowledge and skill must be visible in the curriculum lest we appear to be moving the target, especially for non-privileged groups that have spent years trying to figure out just what it is they must do to succeed in schools. Curriculum reform proposals that ignore this issue are, incidentally, neither progressive nor child-centered since they work against the very people they are intended to serve.

This last guideline may appear to contradict others. How is it that I can simultaneously call for serving the interests of young people and democracy while also insisting that we enhance those skills that are required by external and sometimes undemocratic sources? Given my argument about non-privilege and the denial of access, the problem here is not one of contradiction, but of tension. That is, so long as those external pressures maintain their power, we are faced with the "tense" need to facilitate self and social meaning without inhibiting future possibilities for early adolescents. Teachers and other educators thus face the problem of striving for balance between these two sources of the curriculum, an uneasy balance that is, incidentally, one among the many concerns of those who are working toward curriculum integration.

These guidelines are intended to sketch out what might be characteristics or qualities of a middle school curriculum. Although there are clear implications for such things as student participation in curriculum planning and the use of themes to organize the curriculum, the guidelines do not present a technique or a method. Nor do they say what the actual curriculum ought to be. The point is that in any particular middle school we might see a curriculum in action that is different from that in other places. But whatever that curriculum is, it would bring these guidelines to life.

Before leaving the guidelines I want to make two more points about them. First, notice that I have not called them characteristics of a "good" middle school curriculum. If we think about it, a curriculum that ignores these guidelines is quite simply not a "middle school" curriculum. It may be a curriculum for some other purpose or group, but not for the middle school. We do a disservice by talking of a "good" middle school curriculum since we thus imply that some other curriculum, even though it may be not as "good" or even outright inappropriate, may still be considered a middle school curriculum. Why would we want to be working with or even considering anything that is not good?

Second, these guidelines imply that middle school curriculum conversations ought to involve more than just middle school talk. While the middle school movement has been partly about reclaiming the historically degraded self-esteem of those who work at this level, we must be careful not to isolate ourselves from the larger purposes of schools or the issues that confront them. For example, conversations about democracy, human dignity, and cultural diversity belong in the middle school but are more than just "middle school" talk. The same goes for issues like testing, national curriculum, school legislation, subject area pronouncements, and the like.

-------------------- **❝** --------------------

We must be careful not to isolate ourselves from the larger purposes of schools or the issues that confront them.

In the end, though, it is the guidelines that I have sketched that drive the rest of this volume, just as they do the many middle school curriculum conversations that are emerging and the work of concerned middle school educators in a growing number of places. For those who read through this entire book, I recommend coming back to this section in the end to remember what our curriculum conversation is meant to be about.

Summary

Despite the progress made in the thirty years of the middle school movement, it can be viewed in some ways as very contradictory. Persistent claims about the need for sensitivity to the characteristics of early adolescence have resulted in important organizational changes, but little has been done to answer the crucial question of what ought to be the middle school curriculum. This situation probably had more than a little to do with the fact that the middle school was originally seen primarily in terms of school reorganization and secondarily as a comprehensive school reform effort.

The problem of curriculum reform in middle schools is compounded by the fact that they, like other schools, are subject to many pressures: external curriculum mandates, expectations of parents and the society, the structures of tradition, the interests of subject area specialists, theories and proposals about middle school reform concerns and interests of local educators, and the expectations of local early adolescents. Difficult as curriculum reform may be under any circumstances, the fact that these pressures present competing and conflicting interests makes the matter of rethinking the middle school curriculum thoroughly problematic.

Many middle schools have reacted by framing a fragmented curriculum that attempts to respond to all of these interests in one way or another. In doing so however, it has failed to conceptualize a broad and coherent answer to the question, "what should be the middle school curriculum?" Surely middle school educators must sense in their work a persistent tension between the school and early adolescents that sensitivity and organizational changes have failed to resolve. While this tension may well reside in complicated issues involving the society and schools in general, it is also likely that it is at least partially located in that curriculum question.

Progress toward creating a genuine "middle school" curriculum must begin with serious conversations about the curriculum questions as well as classroom adventures to bring those conversations to life. This is not, however, work in which "anything goes." While there is no specific map, there is a compass to guide us. This compass amounts to guidelines that suggest a middle school curriculum ought to have certain qualities: a focus on general education, the exploration of self and social meanings, respect for the dignity of young people, grounding in democracy, prizing of diversity, personal and social significance, life-like and lively content and activities, and rich opportunities for enhancing knowledge and skill. How the actual curriculum looks may be as diverse as there are middle schools and classrooms. Wherever we go and whatever we may see in the name of "curriculum, though, we ought to see those guidelines brought to life in the school experiences of early adolescents.

2.

Curriculum Views in the Middle School Movement

The question of what "ought" to be the middle school curriculum has not been entirely neglected in theory and research associated with the middle school movement. In the relatively short history of the movement, a few theoretical proposals have been advanced and some local reports made indicating occasional progress in middle schools themselves toward seriously rethinking the curriculum. However, in this chapter we will see that for the most part the proposals have been framed within the separate subject area tradition while the overall curriculum picture in many middle schools remains confused. To explore this situation we will turn first to theoretical statements supplied by some of the leaders in the movement and then go inside the schools themselves.

Curriculum ideas

Donald Eichhorn, one of the early advocates of the middle school movement, worked out a proposed curriculum organization that attempted to deal with the movement's persistent claim that the curriculum ought to be based upon the characteristics of early adolescents. In *The Middle School* (1966), a classic work reprinted by the National Middle School Association and the National Association of Secondary School Principals, Eichhorn concluded that a study of those characteristics suggested a "two curricula" model in which all middle school students should be involved. One, the "analytical" curriculum, would engage learners in the "universality of mental thought processes" (p. 72), particularly in terms of the Piagetian types of reversibility and associativity. A second, the "physical cultural" curriculum, would emphasize aesthetic, social, practical, and physical areas, preferably in some integrated form.

Compelling as Eichhorn's case may be, however, his proposal presents one of the continuing contradictions in middle school curriculum theory. That is, having carefully described the characteristics of early adolescence, and having conceptualized what is apparently an appropriate "curriculum" design, he proceeded to parcel out the the two "curricula" into traditional subject areas. The analytical part was given over to language, mathematics, social studies, and science while the physical-cultural components involved the categories of fine arts, practical arts, cultural studies, and physical education. In short, this was not a new "curriculum" proposal but rather a theory of how what is usually taught in middle schools might be seen in light of early adolescent characteristics. The subject curriculum itself had not changed, only the way in which it was conceptualized.

In a widely read book, *The Emergent Middle School,* William Alexander, another pioneer in the middle school movement, and his colleagues (1968), sketched out what they thought ought to be the curriculum organization for the "new" middle school. In their view, the curriculum needed to be classified into three categories of "learning opportunities": personal development, skills for continued learning, and organized knowledge (p. 65). Personal development included counseling and referral through home-based and specialized services, development of values, health and physical development, and individual interests. Skills for continued learning included reading, listening, interviewing, observing the natural and social environment, evaluating information, problem solving, and more, addressed in all classrooms and through specialized instruction and independent study (p. 72). Organized knowledge consisted of subject matter in the areas of English, mathematics, science, and social studies.

In this work, then, we find what is still generally thought of as the classic curriculum organization for the middle school. Personal development is addressed through home-based or advisory groups and individual interests through an activities program. Various skills are developed consistently across the school and specifically in special skills development programs. And, of course, the "big four" academic subjects are given a central and prominent place in the overall program of the school. The idea of interdisciplinary teaming, which was destined to become a hallmark of the middle school movement, was, in Alexander's work, not so much a curriculum aspect or possibility of the school, but an organizational structure or staffing pattern alongside self-contained, single subject team, and similar arrangements. That way of categorizing interdisciplinary teaming, with emphasis on "teaming" rather than "interdisciplinary," was clearly a harbinger of things to come.

Theodore Moss (1969) envisioned a somewhat different curriculum organization for the middle school based upon a four area design. The first area included development of skills in language arts, computation, and library use through an individual approach. The second focused on a combination of a "core" curriculum, based on personal and social issues, and study in subject areas. This area was to emphasize concepts and understandings with the assumption that skills would be taken care of in the first area. The third area involved what Moss called "the arts:" art, music, drama, and industrial arts. The fourth included health education, recreation, and physical fitness.

Ironically, though Moss noted the growing disenchantment with junior high schools in the opening chapter, the curriculum design he described included most of what had become the typology for many junior high schools, a not unexpected design given the general lack of attention to the curriculum question in those years. Clearly the four standard academic subjects retained their central place in the curriculum although the addition of a problem-centered "core" offered a different view of general education. Placed together they would presumably have a peaceful and balanced coexistence in the middle school. Beyond this, the exploratory or "arts" areas occupied their typical secondary place in the curriculum and the matter of trying to balance concepts and skills in subject areas was handled neatly by teaching skills in a separate part of the program. That the exploratory areas might play a more crucial role in the curriculum or that skills might best be learned in the context of ideas continued, in this work as in others, to escape theoretical thinking about middle level curriculum.

These three curriculum treatments from the early days of the middle school movement were still full of what had largely been the typical program of the junior high school. The authors all described the characteristics of early adolescence, particularly Eichhorn, but it is not at all clear that the "curriculum" designs they proposed were really responsive to those characteristics. At best, each proposed various pieces of the curriculum to match particular developmental dimensions of early adolescence. The power of personal-social aspects of this stage, so often cited by middle school theorists, was not to receive serious consideration until John Lounsbury and Gordon Vars published A *Curriculum for the Middle School Years* in 1978.

Lounsbury and Vars, like others, reviewed the characteristics of early adolescence but concluded that the personal-social dimensions ought to have a larger place in the curriculum. The centerpiece of their proposal was the idea that "a major portion of the common learnings should be provided through a core program, most simply described as a problem-centered block-time program" (p. 46). This program would include "much, but not all, of the content and skills traditionally taught in English, social studies, and science classes," as well as art and music, "so often relegated to a peripheral role" (p. 46). Supplementing the "core" were a "continuous progress" skills development program, including skills and concepts in science, reading, mathematics, and foreign languages, and a "variable" component involving independent study, interest activities, and other "loosely defined" areas.

In emphasizing a problem-centered core program, the authors continued their own work (Van Til, Vars, and Lounsbury, 1961) as well as that of others (Faunce and Bossing, 1951; Hopkins, 1955; Gruhn and Douglass, 1956; Zapf, 1959; Hock and Hill, 1960; Alberty and Alberty, 1962) that referred to this arrangement in a variety of ways including "unified studies" and "common learnings." At the same time, they also maintained the overall program proposal of that tradition by supplementing the "core" program with additional work in separate subjects. Popular and sensible as the core program was in theory, like other proposals that suggest a repositioning of some content away from traditional subject areas, it did not exactly receive an overwhelming response from junior high schools.

As Grace Wright had found in a 1958 survey of United States junior high schools, about 19 percent had a block-time program, but only about 12 percent organized the block around a problem-centered approach. Meanwhile, the rest used a block-time arrangement, but the organizing pattern simply included two or more separate subjects or some modest correlation between them. Given these data from the halcyon days of the junior high school, it was hardly surprising that the Lounsbury and Vars proposal was met with little enthusiasm in its own time. Indeed, Bernard Gross found in a 1972 survey of middle schools that about 40 percent of those reporting some kind of block program also indicated that subject areas retained their distinct identity in the block. Clearly the major concern in middle level "reform" has been on the organization of time and other institutional features rather than on the curriculum.

――――――――― **❝** ―――――――――

The major concern in middle level reform has been on the organization of time and other institutional features rather than on the curriculum.

A telling example of this problem is evident in the widely read volume by William Alexander and Paul George (1981), *The Exemplary Middle School.* The authors pointedly indicate the failure of the separate subject approach to the curriculum and offer several alternatives including use of a problem-centered core as described by Lounsbury and Vars. However, they place this within the context of teacher planning arrangements and, moreover, end up favoring modification of subjects in the context of "domain-centered" planning such as Eichhorn's. Clearly, unless the view of alternatives begins with the fundamental purpose of middle schools themselves, it is most difficult to imagine a substantially different curriculum form in practice.

The contradictory status of middle school curriculum has not gone altogether unnoticed. For example, Leslie Kindred et al. (1981) pointed out that while "the middle school represents a new approach to education for the middle years...conventional subject matter areas not only provide the content for most middle school curricula, but also help to define scope" (p. 67). That the authors did not thereafter describe an alternative curriculum form is, however, typical of the "curriculum hole" in middle school theory.

While this may seem to be an overly dramatic statement, a look at more recent sources on the middle school suggests that it is not altogether inaccurate. For example, in a N.S.S.E. yearbook entitled, *Toward Adolescence: The Middle School Years* (Johnson, 1980), almost everything but curriculum was addressed. The widely read *An Agenda for Excellence at the Middle Level* (NASSP Council on Middle Level Education, 1985) described several desirable curriculum goals and instructional characteristics, but not the curriculum itself. Perhaps most revealing, though, is that even in *Perspectives: Middle School Education, 1964-1984* (Lounsbury, 1984), a remarkable collection of essays by many of the leading figures in the middle school movement, the matter of curriculum was treated in a few scant pages. And here, the only alternative to the subject approach was a set of humanities and technology themes that might be addressed by combining various subjects (Compton, 1984, pp. 75-77).

There are, of course, exceptions to this trend. John Arnold (1985) suggested that five principles ought to be considered in developing a responsive curriculum for emerging adolescents. These included (1) helping students with the task of understanding themselves and the world, (2) using developmentally appropriate methods and materials, (3) emphasizing "knowledge, not simply information and isolated skills," (4) focusing on concrete and real world experiences, and (5) trusting the instincts of experienced teachers to plan and carry out the curriculum. Edward Brazee (1987, 1989) called for a rethinking of the typical middle school curriculum and pressed for a broad conceptual base rather than a narrow focus on fragmented subjects. While these two theorists have mainly critiqued the current middle school curriculum, their work comes as close as any to indicate possible grounds for authentic reform.

Meanwhile, Vars (1987) has more recently restated the case for a problem-centered approach to the curriculum while an issue of the *Middle School Journal* (August 1987) was devoted to examples of thematically based correlation units. And in a very dramatic way, Chris Stevenson (1986) has described practical experiences that combined early adolescent inquiries into their own concerns with an opportunity for teachers to learn more about the young people they work with.

However, these exceptions illustrate an important point. They tend to emerge in the work of only a few middle school theorists and otherwise by teachers who have experimented with alternative curriculum possibilities, typically in relation to interdisciplinary units. Moreover, the latter are unusual enough to be cited as "exceptional" examples of middle school practice.

――――――――― **"** ―――――――――

Curriculum change is a weak link in the chain of concepts that constitutes the middle school movement.

Now it is certainly the case that teachers are quite capable of creating curriculum theory out of specific teaching-learning situations. However, if their case reports are exemplars of curriculum possibilities, we might expect the conceptual ideas behind such practice would enter the more general theory of the middle school or at least the work of more than a handful of so-called "theorists." Perhaps calling this a problem of the "curriculum hole" is a bit of an overstatement. Maybe it is better to say that curriculum change is a weak link in the chain of concepts that constitutes the middle school movement. But whatever we call it, the development of a broadly conceived and reasonably coherent conceptualization of the middle school curriculum is clearly an area of serious neglect.

Curriculum practice

While curriculum rethinking has had a limited place in the middle school movement generally, its place in actual middle schools is even more problematic. As we have seen, while particular cases of alternative forms have been reported from the schools, they hardly represent the usual case of practice. Returning to the surveys of Wright (1958) and Gross (1972) we may assume that the majority of schools in the middle have continued the separate subject organization despite theoretical suggestions for alternatives and empirical evidence to support them.

At the harshest extreme we can undoubtedly characterize much of
what passes for "curriculum" today in much the same way that the
Educational Policies Commission (1938, p. 147) did some fifty years
ago:

> Setting: a democracy struggling against strangu-
> lation in an era marked by confused loyalties in the
> political realm, by unrest and deprivation, by much
> unnecessary ill-health, by high-pressure propaganda,
> by war and the threats of war, by many broken or ill-
> adjusted homes, by foolish spending, by high crime
> rates, by bad housing, and by a myriad of other,
> urgent, real human problems. And what are the chil-
> dren in this school, in this age, in this culture, learn-
> ing? They are learning that the square of the sum of
> two numbers equals the sum of their squares plus
> twice their product; that Millard Fillmore was the
> thirteenth President of the United States and held
> office from January 10, 1850 to March 4, 1853; that
> the capital of Honduras is Tegucigalpa; that there
> were two Peloponnesian Wars and three Punic Wars;
> that Latin verbs meaning command, obey, please,
> displease, serve, resist, and the like take the dative;
> and that a gerund is a neuter verbal noun used in the
> oblique cases of the singular and governing the same
> case as its verb.

We may quibble over the particular examples used by the Educational Policies Commission or say that they are out-of-date, but the fact
remains that the essence of the curriculum suggested is still with us in
many middle schools today, as well as in ideas about "cultural literacy"
(e.g. Hirsch, 1987). More recently Lounsbury and others (Lounsbury,
Marani, and Compton, 1980; Lounsbury and Johnston, 1988, Lounsbury
and Clark, 1990) have carried out classic "shadow studies" of early
adolescents in middle schools and if their reports are read through a
curriculum lens, many if not most classrooms continue the tradition of
simply accumulating and storing facts.

What passes for "curriculum" in many middle schools is, in fact, at
exactly that level. Often, for instance, the curriculum is actually a

vocabulary test: that is, the "learning" of the terms that constitute the language of various subject areas with little or no concern for the meanings they form and the understandings they involve. Arithmetic exercises are repeated from year to year, taught in the same ways that they were or were not learned before. Names of explorers are memorized along with the lands they "discovered" and the routes they traveled, for no apparent reason other than that they will appear on this year's version of the same test that is given every year. Sentences are diagrammed and obscure parts of speech memorized, as if such exercises constitute the essence and spirit of the writing process. And when questioned, such a "curriculum" is defended on the basis that these "learnings" will be needed later on, though exactly where is not clear, except, perhaps, in other classrooms where they will likely be taught again in the same or similar form.

But what of the much heralded use of interdisciplinary teams in the middle school as well as other instructional arrangements often talked about? Here we run into the recurring contradiction between organizational restructuring and curriculum reform. The fact is that interdisciplinary teaming is seen largely as a staffing pattern that provides teachers with opportunities to interact with one another. I do not want to question the need for such interaction, especially at a time when centralized educational planning has contributed to the de-professionalizing and "de-skilling" of teachers (Apple, 1986).

Interdisciplinary teaming does not necessarily lead to interdisciplinary curriculum organization.

However, experience tells us that interdisciplinary teaming, with all of its possibilities, does not necessarily lead to interdisciplinary curriculum organization. My own conversations with "team" teachers suggest that they spend the overwhelming majority of their time talking about individual student problems, disciplinary procedures, and logistical-administrative issues. While these are not unimportant topics, they are not central curriculum considerations. Indeed, the fact that the first two are often "effects" of the typical curriculum illustrates that such deliberations are "reactive" rather than "proactive" curriculum gestures.

Moreover, what interdisciplinary teaching does take place is consistently of a particular kind, namely "simple" correlations of subject areas. For example, many teams undertake thematic units, including the ever popular "colonial living" unit, in which various subject areas make subject-specific contributions during some part of the unit. However, the subjects retain their distinct identity in the units and the contributions often depend upon how much time particular teachers want to devote to them in relation to other content they "need" to cover in their subject. In this sense, such efforts, salutary as they may be, might more accurately be called "multi-disciplinary" (Meeth, 1978; Jacobs, 1989). From a historical perspective, they resemble what was called a "broad fields" approach (Faunce and Bossing, 1958) and thus stop short of possibilities for integrating information from different subjects within themes that transcend the subjects themselves (Beane, 1976).

---------------------   **"**   ---------------------

**What interdisciplinary teaching does take place
is usually simple correlation of subject areas.**

Beyond that kind of subject correlation, many teams also attempt to coordinate skill development across subjects. A language arts teacher may review writing skills involved in preparing an essay for social studies class or teachers on the "team" may simultaneously ask students to use the same study skills in each subject. Again, though, such skill coordination is not really about curriculum reorganization. Instead it is about trying to increase the possibility that what has always been taught will more likely be learned this time around, a not altogether false expectation as some evidence on middle school "success" indicates (George and Oldaker, 1985).

Even from the standpoint of curriculum correlation, however, interdisciplinary teaming has created, or perhaps reinforced, a perennial curriculum problem in the middle school. As typically practiced, teams consist of one teacher each from language arts, social studies, science, and mathematics. To support cooperative planning among these teachers, a period of time is scheduled each day so that they might meet. And where do the students go during his time? They go to the "special" or "exploratory" subjects like art, music, physical education, industrial arts (a.k.a., technology), and home economics (a.k.a., home and career skills). In other words, curriculum "correlation" is not for all subjects, but rather the "big four" that make up the "academic" portion of the program. Thus the possibilities for comprehensive correlation across the whole school are immediately limited.

Admittedly, "team" teachers sometimes "involve" these other teachers in particular units, but that involvement is typically based upon traditional notions of what happens in them. During the venerable colonial living unit, the home economics teacher might be invited to make colonial clothes with students or cook colonial foods, thus reinforcing the usual idea of what teachers in home economics might be interested in or what their area really involves.

Meanwhile, to stay with this example, many home economics teachers are seriously engaged in curriculum thinking about such topics as communications, human development, family crises, values analysis, and other issues that loom large in the real world of early adolescents and their cultures (Staaland, 1987). Ironically, then, even as the middle school has self-consciously sought to raise its own status in the larger educational organization including its claims for interdisciplinary instruction, its own "reformed" structure has simultaneously solidified the second-class status of some of those within its own walls .

The contradictory nature of interdisciplinary teaming was perhaps best described by Vars (1966, p. 262) when he said that, "far from being the 'salvation' of core [curriculum], team teaching may prove to be the Devil in disguise." What middle school teachers have learned over the past decades is that usually if they are "nice" to early adolescents, if they use such methods as cooperative learning, if they engage students in projects, and if they keep a close eye on how individual learners are doing, then they can get away with almost any content. The echo of this discovery rings in a statement about social studies in the middle school: "The authors believe that the crucial decisions at this level are instructional not content"(Bragaw and Hartoonian, 1988). Certainly these procedures are very important and I do not want to denigrate them in the least. Yet they also serve to continuously obscure the larger curriculum question. Nor do I mean to blame this state of affairs wholly on teachers and other local educators since they are often caught up in the very web of competing curriculum regulations and expectations I described earlier; such would simply blame the victims.

Perhaps blame should not really be placed anywhere in particular. Perhaps it should be placed in many directions. But if pressed to the point, we might well look long and hard at the middle school movement itself, the symbol of middle level "reform," that has obviously failed to name or attach itself to any compelling vision of what the middle school curriculum really ought to be.

Summary

The curriculum question has not gone entirely untouched in the middle school movement, but neither has it been answered in a satisfactory way. Several theorists in the early days of the movement proposed "new" curriculum designs based upon the characteristics of early adolescence, but typically, after reciting those characteristics, various dimensions were parceled out into familiar subject areas. From a theory standpoint, only the idea of a "problem-centered core," a semi-popular arrangement from the "salad" days of the junior high school, has continued as an alternative to the subject area curriculum.

A few theorists have recently offered careful critiques of the typical middle school curriculum and while not filling out alternative possibilities, they have laid important groundwork for such work. So too have some teachers pushed beyond the "typical," particularly in constructing thematic interdisciplinary units. Aside from these, recent "theory" regarding middle school curriculum has focused mainly on curriculum goals and instructional processes while middle school practice continues to be confounded by the deadening effects of low level subject area instruction.

It is in this picture of the current status of middle school curriculum, in both theory and practice, that we find the most frustrating aspect of the middle school movement. Despite all of the progress that has been made within the movement, it has yet to include a compelling, coherent, and broadly conceived conception of what *the* middle school curriculum ought to be. The case is not unlike that which Andy Hargreaves (1986, p. 6) describes in speaking of the middle school movement in England:

The appeals to sentiments of unity and balance
while having a consensual tone and arousing a sense
of common purpose, were also unhelpfully vague,
abstract and generalized. They lacked clear reference
points, distinct indications of the shape middle school
ought to take.

In the next chapter we will look at part of the reason behind this
dilemma, namely the ambiguous meaning of general education and the
relentless pressure of those who advocate the predominance of the
"academic" subject area approach.

3.

The General Education Question at the Middle Level

The question of what ought to be the middle school curriculum is problematic for a number of reasons. Not the least of these is the place of middle level education in the historical development of schooling. Prior to the time when junior high schools were formed, beginning around 1910, many educators had recognized that in the K-8/9-12 organization, the majority of young people left school sometime between grades six and eight (Gruhn and Douglass, 1947; Van Til, Vars, and Lounsbury, 1961).

Moreover, they believed that six years of elementary-type schooling was sufficient for young people and that academic coursework, particularly that leading to college or work specialization, could be introduced earlier than the ninth grade. For these reasons, many educators believed that it was wise to "cover as much ground" as possible for those who would drop out at that point, that perhaps some could be encouraged to stay if academic subjects were introduced earlier, and that more and better college preparation could be achieved for those who would continue formal education after high school.

In these ways, the "new" junior high school was identified as the initial point of specialization (or "sorting"); even the guidance function in junior high schools of the time was seen largely in terms of vocational counseling (Gruhn and Douglass, 1947). There was, of course, some talk about the characteristics of "pre-adolescents," but it would be overly romantic to assume that this talk was aimed at changing the academic curriculum. Instead, it focused mainly on the idea that these young people were no longer children and therefore "ready" to take on more specialization.

As high school enrollments expanded in the 1930s (aided by the Great Depression, child labor laws, and expanding compulsory attendance laws), the pressure to jam in as much content as possible for potential drop-outs should theoretically have been alleviated. However, the real picture in junior high schools did not change much as the theme of specialization continued. So it was that the junior high school and its curriculum continued to be just that: a "junior" version of the high school (Cuban, 1992).

This problem did not go unnoticed as, for example, Thomas Briggs (1917, p. 289), a founder of the junior high school, pointed out: "The junior high school is an opportunity, not a specific; and unless you have a definite program for reform of the curricula ...I strongly urge you to defer the organization of the junior high schools to your successors."

Meanwhile, some theorists had begun to reconceptualize the junior high school curriculum by suggesting that its central emphasis be shifted from the subject-centered curriculum toward social problems and the emerging needs of early adolescents. At the very least they suggested that a portion of the school curriculum be centered on those themes, a portion that came to be called the "core" program (Gruhn and Douglass, 1947; Faunce and Bossing, 1951, 1958; Van Til, Vars, and Lounsbury, 1961, 1967).

It was this problem- and needs-centered program that they took to define "general education" or that part of the curriculum which addressed the common needs, problems, interests, and concerns of early adolescents and the society. General education was thus differentiated from "specialized education" or the portion that addressed "needs" or interests that were particular to some early adolescents but not of common concern to all. Here, in this "specialized" category, were placed various academic subjects, vocational courses, and so on. As we saw in the last chapter, "core" programs of the kind just mentioned did enjoy some popularity in junior high schools, albeit on a limited basis.

Of interest for the moment, however, is that "general education" was defined in terms of what were taken as common, real-life concerns that were a part of early adolescence as well as those that might arise in the lives of young people because they were and would be participants in a larger society, regardless of what individual paths they might follow. Moreover, theorists argued that since more and more young people were attending high schools and given the fact that early adolescents were not "full" adolescents, it was no longer necessary nor developmentally appropriate to emphasize specialization in the junior high school. In fact, it was suggested that even the specialized portion of the curriculum ought to emphasize "exploration" rather than rigorous mastery (Gruhn and Douglass, 1947).

From a historical perspective, such reasoning was not surprising since the curriculum field in general had begun giving more attention to the developmental characteristics of young people and to conditions in society that revealed deep and serious socio-economic problems. When the spirit of "liberal progressivism" and social reconstruction were combined, a problem- and needs-centered curriculum, as part of an overall experience-centered approach, seemed to be a suitable way to press further toward the possibilities of "learner-centered" schools and more broadly toward democracy and socio-economic justice (see, for example, Hopkins, 1937, 1941; Stratemeyer et al., 1947; Smith et al., 1950; Faunce and Bossing, 1951, 1952; Burton, 1952, Diessel, 1958; Zapf, 1959).

Sensible as this line of reasoning may have appeared to be, it was not the only version of "general education" (again, that which reflects the common "needs" of young people) at work in curriculum theory and practice. Far from it, there were, as always, those who believed that the best general education was a good dose of academic subjects. The power of this camp is best illustrated (then and now) by understanding that one way of defining general education is to ask, "what shall be required of all young people in the school," as opposed to, "what shall be elective?" Needless to say, if we ask that question, the answer was and is, "academic subjects!"

The problem of the subject-centered approach

Even a cursory glance at the history of education reveals the subject-centered approach as the most popular way of organizing the curriculum in schools. Across the twentieth century other arrangements have emerged such as the problems and emerging needs approaches (Kliebard, 1986; Tanner and Tanner, 1980), but none has managed to sway the power of the subject-centered approach for very long. In order to imagine any other kind of curriculum organization it is helpful, and perhaps necessary, to first examine what is behind this approach. In doing so we may also understand why it is inappropriate for middle schools and why it has failed to serve the interests of so many people.

The subject approach to the curriculum, with the "big four" academic subjects as its centerpiece, is the beloved child of a more general view known as *classical humanism*. This view involves the idea that the best education for all people is found in content that has been handed down over the ages in literature, history, and other classical subjects. In fact, even science and some "modern" mathematics were only accepted within this view in the present century (Kliebard, 1986). Today classical humanism is reflected in the organization of curriculum according to a collection of subjects including English, history, mathematics, and science at the center and art, music, and drama (if classical) on the side. It is, of course, a form easily recognizable to almost anyone who has been in a school. And it lives off a view of informational teaching and learning that became unnecessary once the printing press was invented.

❝

The subject approach to the curriculum is the beloved child of a view known as "classical humanism."

While the addition of home economics and industrial arts would almost complete the typical curriculum picture, we must understand that these entered the curriculum by other routes such as the attempt to prepare young people for their predicted roles as "(paid) workers" or "(unpaid) homemakers" and as a compromise between advocates of classical subjects (for privileged young people) and those of practical education (for the nonprivileged).

It is important to remember that the classical subjects were not always simply accepted in their prescribed form. The formation of the "social studies" as an interdisciplinary correlation of history, geography, and other branches of the social sciences reflected interest in bringing this subject closer to the "needs" and concerns of people (Lybarger, 1987; Kliebard and Wegner, 1987). Reorganization of literature, reading, spelling, speaking, and so on into the language arts demonstrated an understanding of the close relations among those areas (Monagha and Saul, 1987). And the development of "general" science and mathematics, while often meant to make these subjects accessible to "non-college bound" students, certainly illustrated the desire to seek practicality out of abstraction in those areas. Yet it is also apparent that the separate parts in "correlated" subjects were and still are frequently taught apart from the whole while particular aspects, such as the history part of social studies, are given privileged status.

The curriculum theory behind the subject approach is quite simply that what is important to know can be found in the content of various subject areas. The underlying learning theory is equally simple: to "learn" what is important to know, one should "study" the content of each subject in turn. So pervasive is this notion that in the negotiated presence of industrial arts and home economics, and later in the addition of "affective education" to the curriculum, even these areas took the form of separate subjects and thus did not violate the theory of the subject-centered approach or the territory of academics.

How did these theories enter education in general and the middle level in particular? To answer this question we must look at several converging forces. First, we must remember the lengthy and powerful tradition of classical humanism and the fact that alternative views, recent as they are, have never had more than a peripheral place in the curriculum. Indeed, the definition of the "secondary" school curriculum was dominated from the beginning primarily by university academics and secondarily by social efficiency "experts" whose interests lay in preparing youth for "appropriate" roles in the emerging industrial society. Interest in personal development and social issues lagged far behind.

Second, we must look back to the power of faculty psychology or mental discipline, a theory that imagined the mind as divided into separate and distinct compartments, each containing particular kinds of information. Working from this theory, curriculum and instruction would presumably aim to "educate" the separate parts of the mind through separate subject teaching. Here, as in the case of the classical humanism curriculum, alternative theories of learning have emerged mainly in opposition to faculty psychology and again only in the relatively recent past. These two taken alone are enough to explain how this approach gained the prominence it has in the curriculum.

——————— **66** ———————

The intellectual elites have been able to insist that the school curriculum look generally like that of the university.

However, that prominence has been sustained by a third factor that is at least as powerful, if not more so. The subject approach that emerges from classical humanism presents the interests of a particular group of people, namely intellectual elites who are mostly employed in universities and whose sphere of concerns is almost always centered on particular "high status" subject areas that are also valued by "dominant" groups in society (Hargreaves, 1986). In this context, they see their own intellectual world as constituting the "good life" and the purpose of education as preparation to enter it, although vocational preparation might be accepted grudgingly for those who are not "destined" to enter that world. To the extent that this view has been accepted by both educators and the general public, the intellectual elites have thus been able to insist that the school curriculum look generally like that of the university. The fact that almost all educators, especially those in middle and high schools, have themselves been "educated" at universities gives even more power to that argument in the schools.

In arguing this point I do not mean to ignore professors in particular subject fields who have raised critical questions about content sources and values in their own areas or, of course, those in fields like education who have resisted domination of the subject approach. In other words, this is not an anti-intellectual statement of the sort made by Sykes (1988) and others. Instead I mean to point squarely at what has been a powerful force in the stranglehold of the subject approach and, secondarily, to remember that even where some academics have raised criticisms within subject areas, those areas themselves are not necessarily questioned.

Within the education profession, then, the subject approach has come to form the basis of the symbiotic or mutually convenient relationship among schools, universities, state departments of education (including certification bureaus), commercial text and testing concerns, and other education "elites." So powerful is this network of relationships that there is barely a recognizable language for thinking about alternatives to the subject approach as the form of general education. It has come to be seen as the way the curriculum is supposed to be organized; it is construed to serve the common "needs" of young people. Other possibilities seem almost preposterous, nearly unthinkable. For example, recent research about middle level curriculum reform (Becker, 1990) has defined "progress" as offering additional and more specialized academic courses. To implement some other approach would apparently require that virtually all of the pieces in the network of subject-based relationships also change, and that event seems almost beyond our imagination.

―――――――――   ❝   ―――――――――

The subject approach presents numerous problems to schools in general and the middle level in particular ... it is alien to life itself.

Dominant as the subject approach has come to be in the curriculum, it is hard to miss the fact that it presents numerous problems to schools in general and the middle level in particular. To begin with it suggests a distorted view of real life as it is commonly experienced by people, including the young and probably most academicians when they are off-campus. Life and learning consist of a continuous flow of experiences around situations that require problem-solving in both large and small ways. When we encounter life situations or problems we do not ask, "which part is science, which is mathematics, which is history, and so on?" Rather we use whatever information or skills the situation itself calls for and we integrate these in problem-solving. Certainly such information and skills may often be found within subject areas, but in real life the problem itself is at the center and the information and skills are defined around the problem. In other words, the subject approach is alien to life itself. Put simply, it is "bad" learning theory.

This should not come as surprising news to educators. After all, we have been getting signals since the early 1940s that the subject approach does not measure up well even in its own claims for appropriate college preparation (Aiken, 1942). In the famous *Eight Year Study* conducted at that time, graduates of thirty experimental high schools fared better in both academic and social measures than did matched peers from typical subject area programs. Most startling, however, was the finding that graduates from the six high schools that varied most radically from the subject approach did better on those measures than all other students, including those from schools that only "tinkered" with the subject approach. Sadly, that report appeared in the early 1940s when people had more important matters on their minds and it was all but forgotten in the post-war years.

On the other hand, we cannot entirely blame preoccupation with a world war on the failure to heed research on non-subject area curriculum approaches. In subsequent years, numerous studies have demonstrated their advantages (Vars, 1992) and it is more than obvious that these, like the *Eight Year Study,* have failed to detract from the dominance of the separate subject organization.

From these two points it is clear that the subject approach is educationally a wasteful way to organize the curriculum. However, with its roots in the classical humanism tradition and its nodding assent to vocational education, this approach offers even more serious problems. The content typically included in subject areas, proposed as it is by intellectual "elites," is based upon a "high culture" view of the world; that is, the classical culture interests of white, upper middle class, and mostly male persons. This high culture view places boundaries on what is considered to be legitimate content for study and has thus "marginalized" all but a Eurocentric view of what makes for worthwhile culture (see, for example, Bloom, 1987, Hirsch, 1987, and Ravitch and Finn, 1987). Even the view of morality typically associated with this white and largely male culture manages to degrade other ways of thinking, including those of women and nonwhite cultures (see, for example, Gilligan, 1982 and Tronto, 1987).

Perhaps this may help to explain why some people find it so difficult to imagine a curriculum of cultural diversity: aside from the usual prejudice, efforts to create such a curriculum are reduced to figuring out how those outside the Eurocentric circles fit into content from which they have been historically excluded. In addition, we should not miss the fact that among the cultures excluded from the classical one are those of young people, a crucial point in understanding part of the tension between early adolescents and the subject-centered middle school curriculum.

In like manner the academic subject approach has also helped to create the incorrect belief that cognition and affect can and ought to be separated in the curriculum (Beane, 1990). In most schools, cognition or thinking is seen in relation to academic subjects and thus anything not "academic" is construed to be the "soft," non-thinking side of the curriculum. In this way, affective dimensions — self-perceptions, values, morals, ethics, and so on — are relegated to separate programs, such as advisory groups, which, in turn are often viewed as little more than a den of base, visceral emotions. Affective dimensions are considered to be non-cognitive and academic subjects, non-affective. That this view is silly is obvious when we understand that in real life cognition and affect are inseparable, a point I will consider more carefully later.

————————— **"** —————————

The academic subject approach has helped to create the incorrect belief that cognition and affect can and ought to be separated in the curriculum.

The faulty assumption that the intellectual, high culture life necessarily defines the "good life" for most people also implicates the schools in another highly questionable practice. When "successful achievement" or "effective schooling" are defined by academic subject mastery, the schools become active participants in the "sort and select" credentialing process that is based upon predictions of future paths that early adolescents may follow in their lives (Apple, 1982).

By now, we ought to recognize clearly that those predictions have very close correlations to class and race positions in the larger society. In other words, the place young people find themselves in according to academic tracks in the school (including the middle school) are very much like the unchanging socio-economic and racial addresses they have on the outside. Thus we must admit that while middle schools are affected by inequities outside the school (a common complaint), it is also the case that those same schools also help to create and perpetuate inequities. Again, we must remember that this situation does not arise from the subject approach alone, but because that approach has its roots in an elitist view of culture and education.

By combining this concept with a bit of historical perspective we can perhaps also understand how the classical academic subject approach gained such widespread prominence in the 1980s. As we were led to believe by the *A Nation At Risk* (National Commission on Excellence in Education, 1983) report that United States schools were in trouble, state legislatures rushed to raise standards and requirements. This action was supposedly related to strengthening the program of the school, which, in turn, would enable the United States to revive its flagging place in the world economy. The definition of the school program that was to be strengthened was the academic portion, a not surprising event given the domination of elite culture academics in educational circles, including the U.S. Department of Education. Not unimportantly, an associated, perceived "problem" was the increasing presence of culturally diverse immigrants who presumably might not sense the urgency of the United States' economic "problem" or share the desire to solve it.

Ironically, this combination of international economic issues and cultural diversity was followed by the same kind of educational "reform" work in the late 1800s, the 1920s, and, of course, after the launching of Sputnik in the late 1950s. In those times, as in our own, the curriculum agenda of the intellectual elites was seen as the way to elevate both the knowledge and the morality of the nation and thus to solve the national "problem." Again, we should have been more surprised if those who already have control over the curriculum had come up with any other alternative. The effects of this view should be particularly obvious to middle level educators since so many found themselves scrambling to hold together innovative arrangements as the academic version of the curriculum was once again pushed down from the high school.

It is at moments like these that we see how the subject approach has paralyzed our thinking about the possibilities for curriculum reform for so long. Its advocates have been very successful at appropriating the meaning of general education and "core" in the claim that the academic life is the good life. And as talk about "restructuring" schools has heated up in the past few years, it is hard not to notice that no matter how "radical" such talk might otherwise be, it almost never touches the sacred subject curriculum. Even in the "progressive" camp of the middle school movement, that talk is nearly all about school organization, sensitivity to early adolescents, and instructional process. It is little wonder, therefore, that the Carnegie report on middle schools called for defining a "core academic program," as if the "core" ought necessarily to be academic, and "improv(ing) academic performance through fostering the health and fitness of young adolescents," as if the physical wellness of young people was not a primary concern in and of itself (Carnegie Task Force on Adolescent Development, 1989, p. 9).

--------------------- **"** ---------------------

**The subject approach has paralyzed
our thinking about the possibilities for
curriculum reform.**

Thus revealed, the subject approach turns out to be a transparent example of an inappropriate and wasteful way of organizing the curriculum in a culturally elite view of the world that marginalizes other views and helps to maintain inequities in society. That it accomplishes the educational effects it claims is not at all clear. It lives off a network of symbiotic and powerful relationship among educational elites. And, in the end, it offers a fragmented curriculum organization with no coherent unity for learning; it is simply a collection of loosely related subject matter understood mainly by academicians. We must understand by this that the formation of the school subjects, the curriculum structure they support, and the relationships they undergird was (and is) the result of a highly political struggle by very powerful groups (Tanner and Tanner, 1980; Kliebard, 1986; Apple, 1986; Popkewitz, 1987; Goodson, 1993). To miss this point is to bypass the fact that the subject approach is, after all, only tenuously defended on educational grounds.

I do not want to imply that all content in typical subject areas is corrupt and worthless. Concepts and skills in these areas include a good deal of what we know about ourselves and our world as well as the ways of exploring meanings and communicating with each other. Instead I want to argue that the usual subject areas do not include all that is known, that they limit our access to broader meanings, and that they present a developmentally and socially poor way to organize the curriculum for general education, which is the central purpose of middle schools. For example, the middle school social studies curriculum is often a lesson in history defined as the chronology of wars and their military "heroes" while the mathematics and science curriculum is a collection of increasingly abstract concepts and skills. Absent or "marginalized" in these examples are the stories of those outside what historians see as the "mainstream" of "important" events, as well as the relation and application of concepts and skills to large social problems and everyday life.

——————— **❝** ———————

The usual subject areas do not include all that is known; they limit our access to broader meanings, and they present a developmentally poor way to organize the curriculum.

From these brief examples, it might seem expedient or even wise to compromise my main argument about the separate subject approach and instead simply argue for a less selective and more practical version of each subject. In this sense, one might argue, as we have already seen, that the problem of the "uses" of knowledge may be answered within the subjects themselves. However, this argument, reasonable as it might seem, still avoids the question of whether the distinction among subjects is appropriate for early adolescents whose view of knowledge organization has first to do with its uses and secondarily with its sources. Surely there must be a better way then — one that begins with the life lived by early adolescents rather than the values of subject area specialists.

Summary

The problematic nature of the middle school curriculum can be attributed to several factors. One of the most important is that even as junior high schools were originally formed earlier in this century, they were seen as "junior" versions of the high school. Despite rhetoric about the special "needs" of early adolescents, the curriculum was focused on retaining potential drop-outs and early academic specialization.

As junior high schools later evolved, the middle level curriculum was reconsidered by theorists who were interested in personal development and social issues. This interest gave rise to needs- and problem-centered core programs as part of the curriculum, albeit on a limited basis. For the most part, the middle level curriculum, like that of high schools, was still dominated by academicians and social efficiency "experts." In these two positions we can easily see the definition of the middle level curriculum as a combination of academic subjects and "special" areas like industrial arts and home economics.

To rethink the middle school curriculum today, we must first understand how the academic, separate subject approach has failed to offer an appropriate view of the curriculum. Problems with this approach emerge from its roots in the elitist assumption that the intellectual life is the good life for all, its faulty conception of how learning occurs, and its "marginalization" of ideas and experiences outside the "high culture" of the upper middle class. In addition, research on this approach has been less than convincing in supporting its claims, even those regarding preparation for college. From this analysis we can begin to understand that the academic-centered, separate subject approach persists mainly on the basis of its strong historical tradition and the symbiotic relationships among educational elites that it undergirds. Its defense is clearly more easily made on political than on educational grounds.

To develop an appropriate version of the middle school curriculum, we must thus reconsider the meaning of general education and then cast the curriculum within that definition. In the next chapter we will see how doing so suggests a defensible version of the middle school curriculum that is more closely aligned with rhetoric concerning what middle schools are supposed to be about.

4.

A Middle School Curriculum

I n this chapter I propose a very different kind of middle school curriculum than the one to which middle school educators, including those who are a part of the "reform" movement, have become accustomed. To illustrate the transition from thinking about the usual academic subjects to a different view of the curriculum, a statement by Jerome Bruner is very instructive. Bruner, some might recall, wrote the popular book entitled, *The Process of Education* (1960), which was to spur many of the subject area improvement projects in the 1960s. Ten years after publication of that book Bruner (1971, pp. 29-30) would say:

> If I had my choice now... it would be to find the means whereby we could bring the society back to its sense of values and priorities in life. I believe I would be quite satisfied to declare, if not a moratorium, then something of a de-emphasis on matters that have to do with the structure of history, the structure of physics, the nature of mathematical consistency, and deal with curriculum rather in the context of the problems that face us. We might better concern ourselves with how those problems can be solved, not just by practical action, but by putting knowledge, wherever we find it and in whatever form we find it, to work in these massive tasks.

Bruner's statement suggests to us a different view of general education than the one based on classical humanism, academic subjects, and social efficiency that has been with us for so long. And it is one that partly underlies the curriculum I want to propose for the middle school. In making my proposal, however, I have tried to be mindful of Dewey's admonition (1938, p. 20): "There is always the danger in a new movement that in rejecting the aims and methods of that which it would supplant, it may develop its principles negatively rather than positively and constructively."

First we must recall the meaning of general education itself. General education refers to that kind of education that focuses on the *common* needs, problems, interests, and concerns of young people and the society. Its counterpart, specialized education, addresses those concerns or "needs" that are particular to some but not all young people. As we have already seen, some people interpret "common" in terms of academic subjects, based upon a belief that the intellectual, high culture life is the right and best life. However, even a cursory glance at early adolescents and the society, as well as how life itself proceeds, indicates that this is a narrow and biased view.

Instead, the *common* concerns of people are based upon two factors. One is the concerns that arise out of the particular stage of life in which people find themselves, such as early adolescence or adulthood. The other emerges from the fact that people do not live in isolation; rather they live in relation to others, both immediate and distant, with whom their lives are inextricably interrelated. For the middle school this means that general education is interpreted in the context of the developmental concerns of early adolescence and the social issues that do and will face these young people because they are living in a social world. And it is this meaning that I believe should define the "core of common knowledge" that the Carnegie Task Force on Adolescence (1989) and other groups have called for.

────────── ❝ ──────────

I want to argue that the middle school ought to be a general education school and that its version of general education ought to be of the kind based upon personal and social concerns.

Now the fact is that early adolescents are not "full" adolescents. This period of dramatic personal-social change involves the "trying out" of roles and values rather than the specification of particular plans suggested by a specialized curriculum developed around academic and "exploratory" subjects. Therefore, I want to argue that the middle school ought to be a general education school and that its version of general education ought to be of the kind based upon personal and social concerns. In order to imagine what a curriculum based on such a version of general education might look like, we must first look at the emerging concerns of early adolescents and then at the social world of which they are and will be a part.

Early adolescence

Hardly a book or journal article about middle schools passes without a statement of the litany of characteristics of early adolescents. My purpose here is not to fully repeat that litany, but rather to sketch out some developmental issues that are a part of that stage. By now, most educators recognize that early adolescence is probably the most dramatic stage in human development in terms of the breadth of physical, socio-emotional, and intellectual changes that occur.

What is not always well understood, or perhaps not acknowledged, is that these are not independent categories nor are they perceived to be of equal concern by early adolescents. Rather they are interrelated and, in the end, physical and intellectual transitions become embedded within the socio-emotional context. Acne, for example, is not in and of itself a concern; instead it becomes a "problem" only when it must be worn in front of peers. If one could hide at home when it appears, one could simply live through it. The development of secondary sexual characteristics is similarly not a compelling concern except in settings like the gang shower where "indecent exposure" is required. Likewise, the intellectual beginnings of conceptual thinking show up not as an abstract category (and not typically in academic courses), but rather in the questioning of adult values, institutional structures, and the like. It is not that these physical and intellectual occurrences are unimportant, but that they are important to early adolescents in particular contexts whose persistent feature is emphasis on personal and social concerns.

Thus it is on those personal and social issues that emerge in early adolescence that we will want to focus part of our attention. As Arnold (1985, p. 14) pointed out:

> Young adolescents are asking some of the most profound questions human beings can ever ask: Who am I? What can I be? What should I be? What should I do? To respond to them effectively, we must forge a curriculum that frequently deals with their own questions...

The issues that these questions imply include, but are not limited to:

1. understanding and dealing with the physical, intellectual, and socio-emotional changes that occur during this particular stage, including the facts about those changes, how they fit within lifespan development, and their implications for personal and social living;

2. developing a sense of personal identity, including a clear self-concept, positive self-esteem, and the ways in which self-perceptions are formed and how they influence attitudes and behaviors in social interactions;

3. exploring questions of values, morals, and ethics in immediate and distant social relationships, and with regard to the form and function of social institutions;

4. finding a place and securing some level of status in the peer group as well as understanding how the peer group forms and operates;

5. developing a personally acceptable balance between independence from adult authority figures and continuing dependence on them for various kinds of security;

6. dealing with the dizzying array of commercial interests that are aimed at early adolescents, including those related to fashion, music, leisure activities, and the like;

7. negotiating the maze of multiple expectations in the home, the school, the peer group, and other settings of everyday life;

8. developing commitments to people and causes in order to form a sense of self-worth, affirmation, achievement, and efficacy.

Again, this list is not intended to be exhaustive, but rather to illustrate the kinds of concerns that are widely shared by early adolescents. In this sense, too, these issues are not simply individualistic concerns that pit each early adolescent against everyone else, including peers. Instead, they are also issues that help to form the collective culture of early adolescents and to connect these young people to others of all ages who share similar concerns about their place in and relation to the larger society. For example, questions regarding self-esteem, social structures, commercial interests, and multiple expectations are not faced by early adolescents alone and certainly not only by any individual in that stage. Thus the self-interests of early adolescents may be seen in relation to the common social interest rather than as a set of purely self-centered concerns.

Moreover, like the social issues that follow, early adolescents would not necessarily be expected to articulate these in this way. However, if we watch and talk to them very carefully, instead of just talking *about* them, we are likely to see these concerns running through a great deal of what they say and do. Regardless of what we might want them to be, the fact is that early adolescents are what they are: young people trying to work through the issues that face them at this time in their lives. They are not simply variables that make up statistical pictures of an abstract category called "early adolescence." Instead they are real people; living participants in an evolving collage of life experiences. Whether the stage-related concerns they have are addressed and resolved has a great deal to do with their quality of life, now and in their futures. The success of a middle school curriculum clearly depends in part on the degree to which it supports early adolescents in this process.

Social issues

The second dimension with which a general education must be concerned is the array of larger social issues that face our society and world today and those which are likely to do so in the future. In conceptualizing this dimension we must remember that early adolescents do not live in isolation within that stage of development or apart from larger realities in the world. Too often they are seen as living only within two roles, early adolescent and student in the middle school. However, in addition to these, they are also members of families, broadly defined; participants in social networks, including the peer group; participants in cultures of various kinds; members of particular socio-economic classes; and, in an odd temporal sense, not just future adults but already partially formed as "adults" by their past experiences (Beane, 1990).

---------------- 66 ----------------

Early adolescents do not live in isolation within that stage of development or apart from larger realities in the world.

Moreover, most of today's early adolescents will live out the greater part of their lives in the twenty-first century and will likely continue to face many of the problems of our own world as well as those now unforeseen that may arise in that future. Obviously these concerns are not necessarily recognized by all early adolescents now, but they do present issues they will face regardless of what paths their lives may take individually. And while such issues may seem more or less remote to some privileged socio-economic or cultural groups of early adolescents, it is becoming increasingly clear that the lives of virtually all are inextricably interrelated in the fate of the common good.

With these facts in mind then, we are in a position to name some examples of social issues that might be taken up within the framework of general education:

1. interdependence among peoples in multiple layers from the immediate network of relationships to the global level;

2. the diversity of cultures that are present within each of those layers, formed by race, ethnicity, gender, geographic region, and other factors;

3. problems in the environment that range from diminishing resources to disposal of waste and that come together in the question of whether we can sustain a livable planet;

4. political processes and structures, including their contradictions, that have simultaneously liberated and oppressed particular groups of people;

5. economic problems ranging from securing personal economic security to increasing commercialization of interests to the issue of inequitable distribution of wealth and related power;

6. the place of technology as it enters into various aspects of life, and the moral issues it presents;

7. the increasing incidence of self-destructive behaviors including substance abuse, crime, adolescent pregnancies, participation in street gangs, and attempted and actual suicides.

Formidable as this list may appear, it presents only some of the major issues that are located in the larger world and which may be found in present trends and extrapolations of them. To think that these issues are remote from early adolescents is to again miss the fact that they are real people living out real lives in a very real world. Problems like poverty, homelessness, pollution, and racism are not abstract categories for early adolescents; many of these young people experience these problems every day of their lives. Moreover, as we have seen, these issues are "marginalized" by the typical academic-centered, subject area curriculum both in terms of the narrow view of what it presents and by what it leaves out. An adequately framed general education must thus address these issues or risk collapsing under the weight of its own irrelevancy.

The intersection of personal concerns and social issues

If we look carefully at the personal concerns of early adolescents and the larger issues that face our world, it is readily apparent that there is a good deal of a particular kind of overlap between them. As it turns out, concerns in one or the other category are frequently micro or macro versions of each other. Such, for example, is the relationship between developing personal self-esteem and the search for collective efficacy among cultures, between forming peer group connections and pursuing global interdependence, between the status differentiations among peers and the defining conditions of socio-economic class distinctions, between personal physical wellness and environmental improvement, between understanding personal developmental changes and conceptualizing a society and world in transition, and between frustration over adult authority and struggles for human and civil rights.

In the intersections between these two categories, then, we may discover a promising way of conceptualizing a general education that serves the dual purpose of addressing the personal issues, needs, and problems of early adolescents and the concerns of the larger world, including the particular society in which they live. It is here that we may find the themes that ought to drive the curriculum of the middle school as a general education program. And it is here that we may finally find a way of positioning subject matter so that it presents a justifiable and compelling source of study for early adolescents and the adults who work with them.

Figure 4.1 presents an illustration of how this conception of a basis for the curriculum might work. The two outside columns list concerns of early adolescents and social issues.The center column suggests themes that emerge from the intersection of these two sources for various concerns or issues. Themes like these thus present opportunities for integrating personal concerns and social issues, for connecting social issues to the concrete or "lived" experiences of young people, and for developing general education experiences that may extend in both directions. As we will see shortly, it is around themes like these that the curriculum of the middle school may be organized.

Skills in the curriculum

To fully explore themes such as these, early adolescents would need to apply a variety of skills. Among these, of course, are many of the usual skills promoted every day in almost all middle schools, such as communications, computation, and researching. However, since a "living" curriculum calls for more than just "knowing," other, less commonly emphasized skills are also called for. These include the following.

1. **reflective thinking,** both critical and creative, about the meanings and consequences of ideas and behaviors.

2. identifying and judging the morality in problem situations; that is, **critical ethics.**

3. **problem solving,** including problem finding and analysis.

4. identifying and clarifying personal beliefs and standards upon which decisions and behaviors are based; that is, **valuing.**

Figure 4.1
(Sample) Intersections of Personal and Social Concerns

EARLY ADOLESCENT CONCERNS	CURRICULUM THEMES	SOCIAL CONCERNS
Understanding personal changes	TRANSITIONS	Living in a changing world
Developing a personal identity	IDENTITIES	Cultural diversity
Finding a place in the group	INTERDEPENDENCE	Global interdependence
Personal fitness	WELLNESS	Environmental protection
Social status (e.g. among peers)	SOCIAL STRUCTURES	Class systems (by age, economics, etc.)
Dealing with adults	INDEPENDENCE	Human rights
Peer conflict and gangs	CONFLICT RESOLUTION	Global conflict
Commercial pressures	COMMERCIALISM	Effects of media
Questioning authority	JUSTICE	Laws and social customs
Personal friendships	CARING	Social welfare
Living in the school	INSTITUTIONS	Social institutions

5. describing and evaluating personal aspirations, interests, and other characteristics; that is, **self-concepting and self-esteeming.**

6. acting upon problem situations both individually and collectively; that is, **social action skills.**

7. **searching for completeness and meaning** in such areas as cultural diversity.

Where both kinds of skills are presently promoted in middle schools, they are often "taught" in separate parts of the program as if they were distinct aspects of learning and living. For example, compu- tation and researching are included in the "academic" program while self-concepting and valuing are relegated to an "affective" or "advisor- advisee" program. Some, like creative thinking, critical ethics, and social action skills, most often show up only on the periphery of the curriculum, if at all. Such fragmentation misrepresents the realities of life in which all are simultaneously present in thought and action.

In addition, this fragmentation perpetuates the separation of cogni- tion and affect that has dehumanized the curriculum and sterilized subject matter. Broadly defined, "affect" has to do with preferences and choices that arise from our perceptions and beliefs and which emerge in self-perceptions, values, morals, ethics, and the like (Beane, 1990). Cognition, or thinking, is not simply a separate domain; when we think, we think about something. In the case of early adolescents (and most other people), that "something" is most often the affective dimensions of personal and social thought and action and less often the structure of subject areas. Furthermore, while the assumption that cognition is only related to "academic" matters is silly, as we have seen, it also implies the very suspect notion that the present way in which subject areas are "taught" actually involves very much thinking beyond simple recall of facts. The curriculum I am proposing connects cognition and affect and applies them to compelling themes.

Moreover, skills are often taught as if they were ends in themselves; that is, as if skills are isolated categories of learning whose acquisition alone justifies their place in the school program. Yet the fact of the matter is that skills are learned in order that we may *do* something that we believe is important. We learn to read so that we may read about something in order to gain information, understanding or, at times, enjoyment. We learn to compute so that we can figure out problems that involve numeric facts. We learn to analyze and evaluate so that we can look more carefully at ourselves and others.

Because "knowing how" and actually "doing" for some purpose are so closely related, it sensibly follows that skills are only worthwhile when they are actually applied to real situations and, further, that they are most likely to be learned when they are so applied. In other words, the learning and valuing of skills are most likely assured if they are placed in a functional context where their application is immediate and compelling.

Some middle school educators may well argue that many early adolescents do not have these skills and would need to learn them first before undertaking the broad curriculum themes I have proposed. However, this reasoning takes us right back into the isolation of skills from meaningful contexts in which they might be applied. And because isolated skill teaching is so ineffective, this reasoning also promises to continue the situation in too many middle schools where the application level is never reached. A more accurate line of reasoning is that early adolescents may not have these skills for precisely the reason that they have been taught in isolated parts of the program where they are removed from functional application. Moreover, it may be that such skills are sometimes not readily apparent because their "measurement" and the tests for that purpose are connected to the usual subject areas that typically do not engage early adolescents in meaningful ways. In other words, maybe more early adolescents than we think do have certain skills — they just do not demonstrate them in our version of the curriculum.

------------------ **" "** ------------------

Maybe more early adolescents than we think have certain skills — they just do not demonstrate them in our version of the curriculum.

It is also important to note that the view of skills offered here is not based upon a simple utilitarian theory. The variety of skills I have named are not prized only because they have obvious practical use in everyday life inside and outside the schools. Rather they are proposed for that reason and because they are necessary to expand our understandings of ourselves and our world, to create meanings from our experiences, and to extend the possibilities for building a more just and humane world. Difficult as this may be to remember when we are caught up in the everyday exigencies of middle schools, it is, in the end, the only way that we can see that those schools are part of a larger scheme and thus defend their continued existence.

Persistent concepts

So far we have looked at two aspects of a possible middle school curriculum, broad themes that arise out of the intersection of personal and social concerns, and skills that are needed to fully explore such themes. There is, however, one more aspect to be considered if the curriculum is to be complete. Middle schools, like other institutions, do not exist in a vacuum; rather they are part of a society and charged with maintaining and extending the enduring ideas upon which that society is based. While the general curriculum form I am proposing is not meant to apply only to a particular society, the three aspects being discussed here will be seen in the context of societies like that found in the United States that claim their roots in a democratic tradition.

In this context there are presumably enduring ideas that ought to permeate the middle school, including its curriculum. The first is the idea of democracy and its realization in the democratic way of life. The concept of democratic schooling is certainly not a new one since it has been the subject of much discussion in this century and the defense of many school practices, even some that have had the appearance of democratic purposes but undemocratic effects in practice. Most of that talk has had to do with school structures and learning "processes." Ideas like student participation in school governance, involvement of learners in classroom decision-making, cooperative learning, and heterogeneous grouping are obviously related to "democracy" and have been with us for some time. These are, of course, extremely important but as aspects of "process," they do not necessarily raise the question of democratizing the subject matter of the curriculum.

If the idea of democracy is to really permeate the curriculum, then there are other concerns that must be raised as well. For example, the planned curriculum cannot stand on the grounds of "selective content;" that is, subject matter that includes the views and contributions of some people and not others. To be defensible in a democratic society, the curriculum must include possibilities for all views to be heard and for the presence of all people to be recognized. Too often the present curriculum in middle schools, like other schools, reflects the histories and concerns of white, middle class, and mostly male persons. Absent from the typical subject matter are the lives and contributions of "other" persons and in some cases they are altogether invisible. Moreover, as we have seen, the push for "academic" careers reflects the aspirations of only some people and misrepresents the barriers that prevent "others" from entering those careers, as well as devaluing other kinds of work.

---------------- **❝** ----------------

The idea of democracy ought to permeate the middle school, including its curriculum.

Rather than extend this status quo, the middle schools have a moral obligation, rooted in democracy, to open it up for critical examination and broader understanding.

Beyond democratic processes and curriculum inclusion, the concept of democracy also has implications for the uses of content and the construction of meanings. So often, particular pieces of content are brought into the classroom as if they had "sprung from the head of Zeus," absolutely factual and beyond question. If we are to encourage early adolescents to be active democratic citizens, then we must engage them in looking behind the "facts" (Apple, 1979). This means asking questions about particular content like: "Where did this information come from?" "Who said it?" "Under what conditions was it produced?" and, "If we believe this, who benefits?" For example, when someone speaks of the "average person," we might well ask whether there really is such a person. And if posters arrive at the school promoting some moral value or behavior, we ought to ask who produced the poster and why. Ironically, adults constantly wonder aloud why some young people believe everything they read or hear on television, yet this kind of curriculum "habit" does not happen now in their own classrooms.

The point just made refers to knowledge introduced to young people. But if we think carefully about the concept of democracy, it implies that we ought also to recognize and encourage a different kind of knowledge, namely that which young people produce themselves. I am referring here not to some new type of knowledge but rather to he meanings early adolescents construct as they use what is around them to make sense about themselves and their world. A middle school curriculum not only ought to recognize this knowledge in terms of the usual "sensitivity" to early adolescents, but also respect its construction as a moment of democratic action. Put another way, the democratic way of life involves not just the obligation of receiving knowledge but the right and responsibility to make it mean something in our lives.

In this volume I am speaking primarily to the planned curriculum. But of course that can never be completely separated from the "hidden" curriculum — the meanings young people may make from institutional features of the school, its rules and regulations, grouping patterns, grading practices, and so on. This curriculum, too, needs to be scrutinized in terms of democracy. The kind of curriculum I am proposing here seeks to build democratic communities in classrooms and schools. This means that all young people have access to all curriculum possibilities, regardless of their prior achievement or perceptions of their "needs." It also means that all young people have access to success, that there are multiple ways of participating in the life of the classroom and demonstrating knowledge and skill. And it means that the curriculum prizes collaboration and community rather than competition and self-interest. Almost nothing is more unbecoming in a democracy than a hidden curriculum of school practices that is glaringly undemocratic.

----------------- 66 -----------------

The concept of human dignity and the related ideas of freedom, equality, justice, and peace ought to permeate the curriculum.

A second enduring concept that ought to permeate the curriculum is that of human dignity and the related ideas of freedom, equality, caring, justice, and peace. It is here that we may find the subject matter of personal and social efficacy that is now only hinted at in the commercially packaged, contrived collections of self-esteem and human relations activities so often found in middle schools. The formation of subject matter and the ideas it involves are the result of human struggles and human efforts to make meanings out of their experiences. In other words, subject matter is not an abstract, random, or sterile occurrence. Thus, in exploring the broad themes of the curriculum, we must constantly seek human meanings in terms of both the immediate and extended lives of early adolescents. In this way, subject matter may come to life and offer a compelling sense of worth to young people.

A third enduring concept, related to the first two, is the ostensible prizing of cultural diversity. While the history of schooling presents a somewhat bleak picture in this area, we are now at a historical moment when this concept may have brighter prospects. I have already mentioned the matter of selective content that has placed limits on our understandings. But beyond that we must more clearly portray the exciting possibilities of cultural diversity, not only in the sense of the increasing presence of non-European immigrants, but also with regard to the many cultures already present, including the *culture of early adolescents themselves*. A complete and appropriate curriculum must offer opportunities at every moment to explore and appreciate the workings and values of those cultures. And the emphasis must be on the richness of diversity rather than the constricting view of narrow ethnocentrism.

_____ **" "** _____

A complete curriculum must offer opportunities to explore and appreciate the workings and values of diverse cultures.

In naming these persistent and enduring concepts, I have obviously taken the matter of the middle school curriculum beyond the usual middle school talk. No doubt these concepts are somewhere behind some of the efforts to reform the climate and institutional structures of middle schools, but they ought to be more visible in our talk and action. Again, it is only in this way that the middle schools can find a place in the larger society and fulfill their broadest purpose. And it is only by articulating these concepts that the intersecting themes of personal and social living may eventually lead toward an improved quality of life for early adolescents now and in their futures.

A middle school curriculum

To this point we have identified three dimensions upon which the middle school curriculum ought to be based: the themes that emerge from the intersections of personal and social concerns, the skills necessary to fully explore those themes, and the enduring concepts of democracy, human dignity, and cultural diversity. If we now combine those dimensions, we can begin to create a picture of how the middle school might take shape (see Figure 4.2).

The centerpiece of the curriculum would consist of thematic units whose organizing centers are drawn from the intersecting concerns of early adolescents and issues in the larger world. Within the units, opportunities would be planned to develop and apply the various skills I have described, including those usually emphasized in middle schools and those that are often called "desirable" but are typically found only on the periphery of the curriculum. Similarly, such concepts as democracy, human dignity, and cultural diversity would persistently be brought to life in the content and processes used to carry them out.

The centerpiece of the curriculum would consist of thematic units whose organizing centers are drawn from the intersecting concerns of early adolescents and issues in the larger world.

We can begin to imagine early adolescents engaged in a unit on *human relationships* studying the peer group structure in their own school and community, investigating how societies and cultures are formed, exploring ways of promoting global interdependence, participating in community service projects, and interviewing people about how technology has changed their relationships with others.

Figure 4.2
A Middle School Curriculum

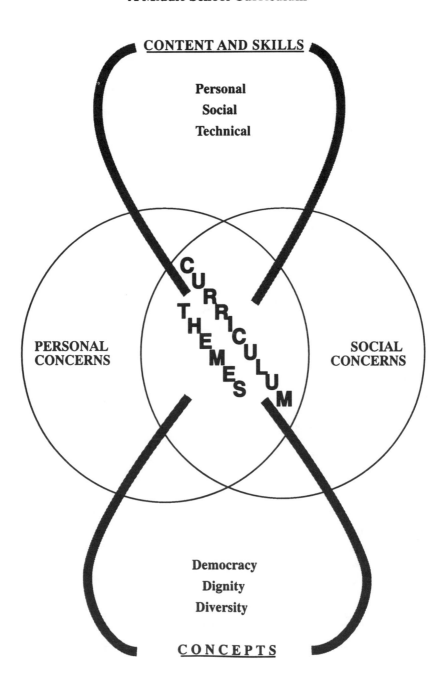

CONTENT AND SKILLS

Personal
Social
Technical

PERSONAL
CONCERNS

CURRICULUM
THEMES

SOCIAL
CONCERNS

Democracy
Dignity
Diversity

CONCEPTS

We can picture a unit on *wellness* in which early adolescents develop a school recycling project, learn about the scientific aspects of pollution, investigate environmental regulations and their relationship to business practices, explore approaches to environmental problems, plot correlations between pollution and health problems in various regions, identify the effects of pollution on their own health, practice the many ways of maintaining physical fitness, and investigate nutrition (including in the school cafeteria).

We can imagine a unit on *living in the future* in which early adolescents develop scenarios on what they consider to be desirable personal and social futures, recommend ideas for improving their communities, learn about biotechnical developments, investigate work trends and forecasts, and debate the moral issues of advancing technology.

We can picture a unit on *independence* that involves examining conflicts between early adolescents and authority figures in the community and school, identifying the causes of past and present national revolutions, analyzing the pressure from commercial media to conform, reflecting on the dependent conditions caused by substance abuse, exploring the tension between dependence and independence in gang customs and behaviors, and studying past and present movements for human and civil rights.

In each case we can also imagine early adolescents reading to get more information, tabulating and displaying data from surveys, researching various ideas, thinking about the consequences of recommendations and decisions, formulating hypotheses, listening to the ideas of others, constructing models, artistically portraying ideas, writing reports, examining ethical issues, and taking personal and collective action to improve their communities. In other words, we can easily imagine how a wide array of skills is continually developed and applied within the functional context of the thematic units that are at the center of the curriculum.

If we look at each case we can also see a great deal of content or subject matter that is presently partitioned out into the various subject areas or disciplines of knowledge — the history of human struggles, the scientific aspects of environmental problems, literature about independence and conflict, the mathematical concepts of distribution and proportion, the artistic and technical design of models, the value dilemmas in family life, the physical dimensions of wellness, and so on. But my argument, once again, is that in an authentic middle school curriculum we would finally not (or need to) see this content as that of separate subject areas. Rather we would see it in terms of themes that arise out of the intersections of early adolescent and larger social concerns; themes in which content or subject matter is seen as transcending the usual subject area lines.

The middle school curriculum as general education

Lest my intention be misunderstood here, I am proposing that the kind of curriculum described above become *the* curriculum of the middle school. To understand how the grounds upon which this stand are staked out, we need to turn back to the idea of general education. Again, general education is defined as that which involves the *common* needs, problems, interests, and concerns of young people and the larger world. It is differentiated from specialized education that addresses the concerns of some young people but not all and, traditionally, those needs that have to do with particular career paths that individuals might follow.

As we have seen, the widely shared concerns of young people and the society clearly are not adequately or fairly presented in the usual collection of academic, "special," and pseudo-vocational subjects that presently make up the typical middle school curriculum. Moreover, early adolescents are not in a reasonable position to make specific decisions about their futures nor are we to make such decisions for them. Thus the middle school ought to be a general education school with a coherent, unified, and complete curriculum that defines "general" upon the basis of what is genuinely of common concern to early adolescents and the larger world.

------------ **"** ------------

The middle school ought to be a general education school with a coherent, unified, and complete curriculum.

In this sense, I am departing from other proposals, such as those cited in the preceding chapter, that recommend a similar version of general education for a part of the middle school curriculum, often called the "core program." On the other hand, it is also the case that the curriculum described here builds from some aspects of those proposals. Historically, these visions of the middle school curriculum call for additional study in separate academic and "exploratory" subjects to supplement the general education "core." In this way, they too kindly accede to the special interests of subject specialists and compromise what *ought* to be done from the start. Besides, our own history at the middle level, including the periodic surveys of school programs cited earlier tells us that those "other" parts eventually wash away the general education "core" in a bath of special interests and academic rhetoric.

This probability is only increased in the typical situation where the middle school is created out of an uneasy combination of elementary and secondary teachers (Hargreaves, 1986). The fact that the latter usually proves to be dominant is aided by the belief that elementary teachers are more "child-centered" and will somehow win over their "academic-oriented" secondary colleagues. That stereotype of elementary teachers is, of course, not nearly so accurate as many people want to suppose as evidenced by the increasing tendency to departmentalize the elementary school and the long-standing practice of using a separate subject or skill approach in self-contained classrooms.

It is important to note, again, that in the curriculum I have described, there is no implication that all of the subject matter and skills usually included in academic and exploratory subjects ought to be cleaned out. Certainly there is much within them that can help in exploring the general education themes and creating personal and social meaning out of them, although just as certainly there are particular facts and concepts often presented that are developmentally inappropriate for early adolescents, culturally narrow, and historically questionable. However, to the extent that academic subjects in particular reflect the "elite culture," we cannot completely abandon their subject matter lest access to educational and occupational opportunities be even further limited than it already is for young people from non-privileged homes. As Apple (1979) points out:

> In short, one major reason that subject-centered curricula dominate most schools, that integrated curricula are found in relatively few schools, is at least partly the result of the place of the school in maximizing the production of high status knowledge. This is closely interrelated with the school's role in the selection of agents (young people) to fill economic and social positions in a relatively stratified society...(p. 38)

As we rethink the curriculum, though, we must be careful not to romanticize the cultures of non-privileged people and thus ignore the extent to which they have often been partially created out of poverty from within and prejudice from without. For example, Leake (1991) and others have raised questions about whether the kind of curriculum I am describing here is simply another "white, liberal" proposal that if implemented would "move the target" just when many non-privileged parents have begun to figure out what their children will need to do to succeed in school. Given much of the history of "innovative" curriculum work, these questions make a good deal of sense. After all, if we walk away from knowledge and skill that are deemed necessary by dominant forces in society, then a "new" curriculum, no matter how theoretically attractive, will only backfire on non-privileged young people.

The curriculum I am proposing repositions much of "traditional" content within the context of personal and social themes where it becomes what is known and prized. For example, it may well be that the classical European literature that so often takes up all of the space in English/language arts courses can offer a source of insight and meaning in relation to particular themes. However, so can non-European and non-upper and middle class literature and, of course, the literature that early adolescents themselves produce in both formal and nonformal ways.

In like manner, skills "traditionally" emphasized are also repositioned. For example, we cannot ignore arithmetic or computational skills since they are helpful in many ways as we find, analyze, and solve problem situations. Here, though, they are not seen as isolated or self-justified skills, but rather as functional skills, developed and used in the context of important themes under consideration. For example, adequate work on almost any theme would call for tabulating data from surveys and graphing results of studies as well as understanding how others have done calculations to arrive at particular conclusions.

Are early adolescents in a position to explore the kinds of themes I have proposed and to exercise the related skills just described? Yes, though obviously not at the same level as some adolescents or adults. Yet as I have pointed out, these themes permeate their lives and, moreover, they are already on the minds of many early adolescents as they begin to raise questions about the world around them and the values it portrays. The central aims of the curriculum I have proposed are to build upon that questioning and to bring the developmental concerns of early adolescence into closer connection with that larger world in a genuinely educative way.

In sum, then, a defensible case can be made for using a version of general education that integrates early adolescent and larger social concerns as *the* middle school curriculum. Clearly such an approach to the curriculum would not only enhance what appear to be the present aims of the middle school, but would also extend and expand those aims in even broader directions. If we use the old adage that "form should follow function," it is also clear that we would need to reconsider various organizational features of the middle school to see how they might support a new approach to the curriculum.

Finding themes and planning with young people

When the first edition of this volume appeared, some readers apparently thought that Figure 4.1 named *the* specific themes around which the middle school curriculum ought to be organized. Instead, I meant these only as illustrations of how personal and social concerns intersect. It is possible, of course, that some of those themes might actually be used, but the matter of finding themes is something that should be done at the local level by those who will carry them out. While there may be many ways of doing this, I will describe two here.

The first involves planning "from scratch" with early adolescents. Elsewhere I have described a guided process used by some teachers in which themes grow out of questions and concerns that young people have about themselves and their world (Beane, 1991, 1992; Brodhagen,

Weilbacher, and Beane, 1992; George et al., 1992). This process also involves working with young people to identify activities and resources related to their questions and concerns as well as the outcomes of their work. This method of planning is particularly promising since it empowers young people and results in organic themes that are framed in terms of their own sense of organization and connections.

For a variety of reasons, many teachers feel reluctant to "let go" in that way. Thus some use a second method that involves teacher identification of themes and then, with variations, involvement of young people in identification of activities, resources, and outcomes. In some cases. young people may be surveyed for possibilities, but theme identification remains in the hands of the teachers. While I am more interested in the former method, I do not want to demean this one since it apparently presents a way for these teachers to try out a thematic approach. However, I am concerned about the kinds of themes that might be identified and the risk of naming ones that are related more to the curriculum already in place than to the kind of general education concepts I have described.

With that in mind, I want to suggest that regardless of how themes are identified, they ought to meet certain criteria (Beane, 1992). Among these are that a theme should:

1. explicitly involve questions and concerns from the young people who will actually carry out the unit;

2. involve questions and concerns that are widely shared among early adolescents;

3. involve widely shared, larger world concerns that are of clear and compelling social significance;

4. engage a wide range of knowledge, skills, and resources;

5. pose opportunities for in-depth and extended work;

6. present possibilities for a wide variety of activities; and

7. present possibilities for personal and social action, both in school and outside the school.

It may be that these criteria are so rigorous that those who use the second method might as well attempt the first, especially since it is hard to imagine that one could know the questions and concerns of early adolescents with confidence short of asking them. But here, again, we must think in terms of the parallel structure to understand that there could be different ways of "asking." Teachers I know who use the first method literally do so on the spot. However, in the case of either method it would be possible to use surveys, to work with a steering committee, to focus involvement of young people on "self" questions only, and so on.

Two ideas are important here. first, the finding of themes is crucial to the curriculum and ought to explicitly involve young people. Second, the involvement of young people in planning does not demean or diminish the important role of the teacher in curriculum planning. Teachers are not just people chosen randomly off the street. They are in schools by virtue of their special preparation for and interest in facilitating the learning of young people. For this reason, even in the first method I described, teachers not only have the right but the obligation to clarify, refine, and stretch the ideas of early adolescents. Besides, teachers too are members of the classroom community and in that role have a right to suggest ways of doing things.

The key idea here is involving early adolescents in the finding of personally and socially significant themes for organizing the curriculum. Unfortunately some critics still mistake such action for simply doing whatever young people want to do. At no place here have I suggested that we ask early adolescents questions like, "What do you want to do?", "What do you want to study?", or "What are you interested in?" Quite to the contrary, my proposal for the curriculum and its planning present a tightly constructed way of viewing the important work we do with early adolescents, one that opens doors for them but in ways that are as pointed and serious as any other.

Rethinking content and skills

Before leaving my central proposal for the middle school curriculum I want to look back once more at the place of content and skill that it envisions. Again, there is no intention here of abandoning all of that which resides within the territories of currently constructed disciplines of knowledge or the school subject areas by which they are represented. The question is not whether there should be content and skills in a "new" curriculum but how those will be brought into the lives of young people.

In cases where young people have been involved in planning, they have identified such themes as "Living in the Future," "Jobs, Careers, Money," "Conflict and Violence," "Environmental Problems," "Sex, Life, Genetics," "Mysteries, Beliefs, Illusions," and "Outer Space." In order to address the many self and social questions related to these themes, it has been necessary to find and acquire a wide variety of content and skills from many sources. In fact, the actual "doings" in these classrooms have looked much like the examples I gave earlier in this chapter. And at any given moment it is quite possible to find the teachers specifically teaching some skill or content from one or another discipline, but always in relation to and because of the theme at hand.

Thematic, non-subject centered units such as these are clearly information and skill loaded, quite often to the extent that teachers have had to reach well beyond their own knowledge and the resources immediately available in the school. The area of mathematics offers an excellent example of how this has worked. In virtually all of the units I have observed or participated in, young people have had to work with statistics — percentages, proportions, ratios, averages, fractions, charts, graphs, and the like. Not only have they had to learn about such statistics but also how to use them to construct and communicate meanings. Here we see that the content and skill of mathematics are not abandoned; rather they are placed in the context of the theme and questions where they take on a new and more vibrant meaning for young people.

In this same way, then, we may sketch out pictures of other areas. Social studies becomes a resource for informing social and historical meanings. Home economics serves as a source of meanings about the family in relation to the economy, work, and institutional structures. Art and music not only offer expressions of meanings by others but ways to express our own meanings. The subject matters of science, industrial arts/technology, language arts, and so on are viewed similarly.

In other words, the question before us is: where can we find what we need to help us take on the questions we have about ourselves and our world so that we might more fully search for self and social meaning?

At the same time, however, I want to add that in such classrooms the knowledge and skills that are sought and used are not done so in the separate categories of subject areas. Instead knowledge and skills are integrated in terms of the activities; they are called forth all at once, simultaneously and without regard for their source. For example, in constructing and presenting a classroom rain forest simulation, students simultaneously use knowledge and skill from a variety of disciplines but do not name these areas as they go along, nor are they asked to do so.

Far fetched as this viewpoint may seem, there are similar movements beginning to appear among subject area groups and various projects associated with them. The National Council of Teachers of Mathematics has recommended that we see their subject terms of communication, exploration, problem solving, and integration rather than as an abstract and strictly skill-driven discipline. The National Council of Teachers of English and the Whole Language movement have in some ways transformed our understanding of what language arts are for and how they might be approached. The National Science Teachers Association and Project 2061 have begun to search for real life themes as a context for their interests. Industrial arts and home economics have been similarly revitalized as having to do with problems of living rather than the narrow pseudo-vocational concepts with which so many people have long associated them.

Perhaps a specific example might be helpful here. Paul DeHart Hurd (1992) had this to say about science:

> The choice of subject matter has been that best suited to illustrate the theoretical structure of selected disciplines, including basic facts, principles, and laws ...the technical language and symbols that scientists use to communicate research findings to other scientists ... The (new) vision of science teaching is one of relating modern science and technology to the realities of our culture, to social progress, to life as lived, and to values we hold. (p. 28)

Heartening as these signs may be, the road to the kind of middle school curriculum I have proposed is still fraught with tensions. For many years teachers at workshops on "interdisciplinary" teaching have been told that they will still "teach" all of the content that they have always been concerned with. Now as we change our view of what the curriculum is about and who and what it is for, that comforting refrain is on tenuous ground. As I have said, this "new" curriculum is knowledge and skill loaded. But that does not necessarily mean that all of what has previously been included will necessarily be retained.

The question of what knowledge or skill might be included in a "new" curriculum must be taken very seriously. The answer(s) cannot be made on arbitrary grounds such as what we do or do not like, what we are or are not interested in, or what one or another special interest group has to say. I think I have made it clear in this volume that we have already had more than enough of that kind of reasoning. Instead we must turn our attention back to the concept of general education, to the idea that the curriculum is for early adolescents in terms of their present lives, to the possibilities of powerful and significant themes, and to the notion of curriculum as a search for self and social meaning.

If we commit ourselves to these concepts, then the answer to the question may well be that the knowledges and skills that are included are those, and only those, that are pertinent to the themes, questions, and concerns that organically (or naturally) arise. On the other hand there may be some questions or concerns that the world poses to early adolescents that they might not see but which we have an obligation to bring to them such as, for example, the issue of cultural diversity in a location that is perceived to be culturally homogeneous. In such cases we might bring such matters to the curriculum as teacher-identified themes or as part of already identified themes (bringing in cultural diversity as young people identify a concern about various forms of conflict).

While this line of reasoning follows naturally from the discussion of curriculum in this volume, it is not always that easy in the real world of schools. After all, there are other discussions about curriculum based upon quite different interests. For example, what happens to algebra, especially if we are unable or unwilling to see it in terms of self and social meanings? What happens to foreign languages? What happens to the favorite yearly unit on the War of 1812 or Ancient Greece? What happens to the unit on rocks and minerals? And even if we can resolve these issues within the middle school itself, what happens when parents, the central office, or the state insists on some other arrangement? Clearly these issues involve not only "curriculum" thinking but political contortions as well.

In the end, the resolution of these issues depends more than a little on how firmly we are committed to a curriculum that is centrally for early adolescents. The curriculum we have now reflects mostly the interests, concerns, and values of adults. If we now introduce those of early adolescents, it is hard to believe that all of what we have traditionally included will survive. This is especially true for those bits and pieces that have found a place as we have played increasingly obscure and abstract games of "academic" trivial pursuit or accommodated the interests of one or another special interest group and the elaborate schemes of scope and sequence that have been constructed around them.

There are no easy answers here, only the prospects for a long and sometimes painful conversation about the middle school curriculum. I have made my own feelings clear but mine is only one voice and I do not have to live and work in the many and diverse places where teachers do. My hope is that as we take on these issues we will be sensitive to the deep loyalties that so many people have to one or another subject area, but finally be willing to place the best interests of early adolescents before our own.

Summary

An authentic middle school curriculum ought to be based on a view of general education that combines the *common and shared* concerns of early adolescents and the larger world. Clearly these are found not in the narrow interpretations of academic, "special," and pseudo-vocational subjects, but rather in the developmental issues of early adolescence and the social issues that do and will face them as participants in the larger world.

In defining these issues it becomes evident that they are often micro and macro versions of each other, a relationship whose intersections suggest compelling themes around which the curriculum might be organized. Such themes allow for several possibilities, among them the integration of personal and social concerns, learning opportunities that may extend in either direction, and an appropriate integration of cognition and affect. At the same time, such themes offer a functional context in which an array of skills may be developed and applied. as well as one in which enduring themes like democracy, human dignity, and cultural diversity may be brought to life.

I have proposed that such units addressing the themes constitute the middle school curriculum. In this sense, even though the idea of a needs- and problem-centered core is not new, I have departed from previous proposals by extending this view of the curriculum across the entire school. Too often, "mixed" proposals have resulted in the demise of the problem-centered portion as advocates of other arrangements have successfully pushed out the "core" and annexed its time in the curriculum.

If we are to believe that the rhetoric of the middle school movement concerning the purposes of middle schools is appropriate, then the curriculum I have proposed is a defensible one. If that rhetoric is sincere, then it is also a logical extension of what those in the movement say is good and right for early adolescents. In both cases, we may now see that the work of the middle school movement is unfinished in very important ways. In fact, as this proposal seeks to answer the middle school "curriculum question," even the organizational components of the school that have received so much attention will need to be reconsidered. It is to this issue that we will turn in the next chapter.

5.

Implementing the "New" Curriculum

Proposals for new and different ways of organizing the curriculum often disappear almost as quickly as they are made. This is partially due to the fact that they immediately get bogged down in a myriad of questions about how to implement them. This proposal is certainly open to such a risk since it is meant to transcend present curriculum practice and to suggest a way of thinking about the curriculum rather than defining specific organizational details. For this reason it does not fit comfortably into the current structure of middle schools; for example, it is not simply something to add onto the school day or, certainly, to slide into one or another subject. Moreover, as we have seen, the fragmented, subject-centered curriculum is so deeply rooted in educational thinking that a new view of the curriculum seems almost impossible to imagine.

I am tempted to leave the proposal stand as it is up to this point and leave the matter of implementation to others, particularly people at the local school level. This would be consistent with the concept of a parallel structure that I spoke to earlier, that is, we should speak broadly of characteristics or guidelines for a new curriculum, but the possibilities for implementation should be taken up at the local level and conceivably be as diverse as there are middle schools and classrooms.

However, given the problems just outlined, the proposal would immediately be "at risk." Therefore, in this chapter I will attempt to sketch out some possibilities for implementation, problems, and alternatives for resolving them. To the extent that the latter may involve serious change, we will want to remember how far middle schools have come in the past thirty years and how the efforts that have created so much progress suggest that almost anything is possible if only we want it enough. We must also understand that the kind of curriculum I have described does not so much ask people to give things up, except perhaps convenience or easy answers, as it does to open up new opportunities for early adolescents and their middle school teachers.

Articulating a different curriculum view

A rush to implement this curriculum proposal would be a mistake just as it would with any other that suggests a genuinely different view of the curriculum. What is initially needed is some serious talk about it. However, this talk cannot be within the middle schools alone. Instead it must also involve educators outside the middle school, parents, and other members of the community, as well as early adolescents themselves. Indeed, unless this way of thinking about the middle school curriculum is clearly articulated and widely supported, its implementation would be doomed to failure as it runs up against what so many people think the curriculum is supposed to be.

In this sense the middle school movement has come to a historic moment in the 1990s. More and more people have come to recognize that early adolescence is a crucial time in the lives of young people and that as they look at data on self-destructive behaviors and school and social alienation, things are not going well for many of these young people. Moreover, the Carnegie Report on middle schools (Carnegie Task Force on Adolescence, 1989) has called national attention to middle level education while numerous states have made improvement at this level one of their top priorities. Ironically, many of the "reforms" called for have been the subject of middle school work for many years and have, in fact, been widely implemented.

At the same time, more and more is being heard about the large issues and problems that our society and the world face — issues like poverty, racism, homelessness, the gap between advancing technology and its moral implications, the crisis in values, the "explosion" of new knowledge, and so on. What this means is that middle schools are currently well-positioned to undertake change, including curriculum change of the sort I have proposed.

―――――――   **"**   ―――――――

If we take the characteristics of early adolescents seriously and see them in the context of present trends in and future forecasts about society the proposed curriculum is logical.

To figure out how talk about such change might begin, it might be helpful to look back on how the middle school movement got started at both the national and local levels. Granted, the main impetus was overcrowding in schools and grade level reorganization to relieve it. But more has changed than just the grade levels included in middle level schools, namely sensitivity to early adolescence as well as many organizational structures of the school. In this case the argument for changing what was happening in middle level schools began with talk about the "kids." For example, the idea of teaming was argued from the viewpoint that clusters of teachers could more carefully watch out for "kids," interdisciplinary instruction was defended on the basis that subject correlations would help "kids" learn, advisory programs were promoted as a way to offer more guidance and a sense of security for "kids," and activities programs were proposed because "kids" have widely ranging personal interests. Given the widespread use of these arrangements, talk about the "kids" can obviously lead somewhere.

In articulating a new view of the curriculum, then, it makes sense that we would turn once again to the characteristics of early adolescents, their relation to the world around them, and their prospects in it. Not only is this politically sound, but it presents the argument upon which the middle school movement has ostensibly been based. Without restating the whole case that has already been made, I will simply repeat here that if we take those characteristics seriously and see them in the context of present trends in and future forecasts about society, the kind of curriculum I have proposed is a logical conclusion.

The articulation of this view must grow out of conversations about curriculum as well as classroom attempts to try out ideas that emerge from them. The former are meant to imagine and clarify new ways of doing things while the latter are intended to create stories that we may tell about what a new curriculum might look like. This, then, is how to get things started. However, I would urge, as strongly as I can, that this initial work be done with volunteers, those who want to do something. Certainly there are some in every school, including teachers, who have previously been tampering with the curriculum behind closed doors and parents whose own school memories make them sense the irrelevancy of the "traditional" curriculum.

In other words, I am pessimistic about real curriculum reform sought at the whole school or district level. Over time we might expect others to join in with this work, but first efforts require high commitment and they are too fragile to leave in the hands of the reluctant. Besides, if we wait for those who are reluctant, or outright resistant, we will all probably go to our graves waiting for something to happen.

As arrangements are made to open conversations with people in our communities it is crucial to seek as broad a level of participation as possible. If the usual approach is used, we are liable to meet only with those whose interests are most heavily served by the academic, subject-centered approach and who are often anxiety-ridden over their children's chances of entering the professions. Certainly we must help these people to see how a new curriculum, by way of its developmental appropriateness and more sensible way of organizing knowledge, would offer greater benefits to early adolescents than the present form. However, we must also do whatever is necessary to involve those who are non-privileged and frequently excluded from curriculum discussions just as they are from the academic curriculum itself. By creating such broad participation we can demonstrate in discussions those interests and concerns that are truly common in society rather than those that emerge from particular class interests.

Planning a new curriculum

In the last chapter I suggested several examples of curriculum themes that might emerge from the intersecting concerns of early adolescents and the larger world. These were meant to be illustrative of this way of thinking about curriculum rather than prescriptions for a new curriculum. This is a very important point for two reasons. First, if the curriculum is to be authentically engaging, then the actual themes used in any particular school must reflect as closely as possible the concerns of early adolescents in that school. Second, middle schools, like other schools, have, over the past decade, been increasingly subjected to centralized curriculum decision-making that has resulted in very serious consequences for local educators: loss of self-esteem and professional efficacy, frustration, lack of commitment, and loss of curriculum planning skills.

For these reasons the actual planning involved in a new curriculum ought to be done at the local middle school level. Early adolescents and their teachers, hopefully with participation by community representatives, ought to themselves gather information about the concerns of early adolescents, carefully study social issues and problems, and subsequently identify possible curriculum themes and related activities. Similarly, those same people ought to consider organizational arrangements within the local school that will support the curriculum. In this way it is quite possible that while different schools may share the same curriculum vision, actual themes, sub-topics, activities, school structures, and the like would vary from school to school.

In describing this kind of curriculum planning and development, I do not mean to imply that it is a simple matter to be taken up in a few after-school meetings. If serious curriculum rethinking is to take place, several issues must be addressed. Those involved would need to have considerable time allotted for such a project, much more than the "tidbits" typically scheduled. Such time and the needed resources for planning and implementation will require money, much more than we are currently willing to spend on the curriculum. And in those situations where administrators and other officials want centralized control over the curriculum and teachers' work, there will need to be a serious shift in conceptions of power so that the curriculum will belong to people in classrooms rather than those in the central office or the state department of education.

Teaching in a new curriculum

While the major emphasis in this proposal has been on the content of a new curriculum, we cannot overestimate the importance of the process of learning. Indeed, as has often been said, the process becomes a kind of content of its own. Here we can turn to some of what has gone on in many middle schools that have pedagogically responded to the characteristics of early adolescents and, though not always deliberately, to the concepts of democracy, dignity, and diversity.

Given the preoccupation over group connections in early adolescence and the idea of collective action that is a hallmark of democracy we might expect that cooperative learning would be of premium value in exploring major themes or subtopics within them. This kind of group work may extend from researching an idea to carrying out a community service project. In doing so, early adolescents might not only see how various issues look through the lens of democracy, but simultaneously experience its workings.

Another important process we might expect to see is collaborative planning among teachers and early adolescents (Beane, 1972; Beane and Lipka, 1986). From the selection of the major theme to the identification of specific activities there are many important decisions to be made. If the new curriculum is to genuinely relate to the characteristics of early adolescents, not as an abstract category, but as the real concerns of real "kids," then it is imperative that those concerns be known. Moreover, the chance to really "have a say" is crucial to developing a sense of efficacy, an idea which is also behind the content of the curriculum I have proposed.

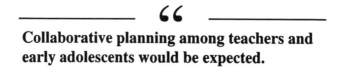

Collaborative planning among teachers and early adolescents would be expected.

As we focus more and more on the questions and concerns of early adolescents it will also be important for teachers to reconceive their role in the teaching-learning process. The concepts of "disseminator of knowledge" and "holder of knowledge" will have to be set aside. Instead we will need to think of ourselves as facilitators in the search for self and social meaning. This means helping early adolescents to pose questions, identify possible ways to respond to them, construct meanings, and reflect upon experiences. Teachers cannot possibly know the answers to all of the questions that might be raised in relation to a theme and so they will also have to begin to see themselves as learners alongside early adolescents.

Part of the role of "facilitator" means, of course, a shift in power relations in the classroom. In this sense the curriculum I have described involves "letting go" of who and what we have become in the old curriculum. But power is not a finite entity nor has it been well-defined in relation to teaching. The old curriculum cast power relations not only in terms of decision-making but also with regard to who gets to define worthwhile knowledge and the value of experiences. "Letting go" of those notions in a new curriculum does not mean giving up power. It is true that as young people develop deeper understandings of themselves and their world they gain greater power over their own lives. In this way, though, the teacher becomes even more powerful in those lives, as a person who has truly made a difference. The rule of thumb is this: power increases for everyone as it is more widely shared among the group.

It is possible that some teachers will say that they are already using these kinds of methods and they may well be telling the truth. However, it is highly unlikely that they are doing so in relation to a curriculum that is different from the typical one. As we have seen, success with "process" or "nice" methods has been one factor that obscured the middle school curriculum question in the first place. Yet I want to be clear that my proposal involves a theory of curriculum, not of "discipline" or classroom management. The classroom is not likely to suddenly be a completely smooth place. Many early adolescents have lives so troubling that they are simply unable to focus clearly on what the school has to offer. And virtually all of us have our "up and down" days. Surely there are possibilities in a new curriculum for more successfully engaging young people in learning, but we must also be realistic. On those days when some students are less than fully engaged in our new curriculum we will still want to ask what is going on in their lives and are we contributing in any way to their alienation, but we will also want to ask, how were they doing before?

In exploring a new curriculum we will likely also rethink the configuration of teachers in the middle school. At the present time, even within interdisciplinary team structures, most teachers think of themselves as subject teachers. If the subject-centered organization is abandoned, this role conception must change. Just as particular content would be repositioned within the context of the major themes, so would teachers be positioned differently. For example, a small group of teachers might stay with a group of early adolescents for all three or four years of the middle school and work through a series of themes with them. Or, some teachers might be aligned with certain themes and thus work on them with different groups of early adolescents. Or, some teachers might work individually with themes in a self-contained setting. Or a small group of teachers might work with a particular theme for a long period of time while others make special contributions on a short-term basis. Or, the whole school might take on a particular theme at the same time with individual or small groups of teachers working with particular parts.

————————— 66 —————————

To implement the new curriculum the role conception of teachers would have to change considerably.

Hard as it may be to imagine this change in teacher roles, we must remember that in this curriculum proposal, the middle school is defined as a "general education" school. For this reason, teachers are not viewed as subject teachers, but as teachers of early adolescents. Where specialized subject knowledge is needed in exploring a particular theme, those teachers who have it may work for a time within any unit. Much more problematic is the matter of knowledge that has been excluded from the selective content of subject areas in the past and which will now come to the surface in the curriculum. I believe that there are many teachers who have such knowledge but have never had the opportunity to use it with young people. By working in collaborative ways with other teachers they may now share more widely what they know.

Finally it is quite possible that some parts of the current interdisciplinary team structures might transfer over to a new curriculum relatively easily. For example, there are still some middle schools that have two or three teacher teams that regularly use a thematic approach during their part of the school day. Moreover, it might be that some "academic" interdisciplinary teams might remain intact so long as they too turn their curriculum over to the major themes. Without question, though, a new curriculum would bring so-called "special" or "exploratory" teachers out of the far reaches of the curriculum and into the mainstream of general education. Indeed, it is very likely that many of these teachers will have much to offer in light of the kind of curriculum they have been engaged in for years.

Grouping

If we correctly define the middle school as a general education school, the pattern of grouping early adolescents heterogeneously is obviously implied. The curriculum I have proposed involves the common concerns of early adolescents and the larger world rather than specialized interests. Since these concerns are shared by early adolescents regardless of ability, school achievement, home background, gender, race, class, personal aspirations, and other characteristics, it follows that there is no need to search for, or mistakenly use, particular characteristics that might differentiate individuals or subgroups from one another.

This view of the curriculum immediately dissolves the argument for homogeneous grouping based upon academic differences among early adolescents that has been so hotly contested in recent times. Interestingly, the debate over heterogeneous versus homogeneous grouping has been waged mostly on the grounds of academic advantages or disadvantages to one group or another and less often with regard to affective outcomes. Yet as Jeannie Oakes (1987) and others have so forcefully pointed out, the real argument against homogeneous tracking is found in the disproportionate presence of poor and non-white young people in the lowest groups or tracks.

That these young people have the same unchanging address in school as they do outside is an example of how the school helps perpetuate and create inequities in the larger society. Moreover, in the present proposal we may also see how this kind of prejudicial grouping grows out of the continuing use of a subject-centered approach while the debate in that context only helps to further obscure the question of whether the curriculum itself is partly at fault in both the broad sense of social inequities and in the sense of artificially creating "differences" among early adolescents.

Can the kind of curriculum I have proposed account for individual differences and appeal to varying abilities and interests among early adolescents? If we look carefully at even the few examples I gave, it is obvious that the exploration of any theme would offer a wide array of possibilities and opportunities to pursue subtopics of many kinds to various depths and in many ways. For example, small groups might take on different or the same topics and, depending upon interest, thereafter investigate different angles on their topic to whatever extent they choose. In these settings, such labels as "gifted" or "learning disabled" would have no meaning since they are products of the subject curriculum and adult value systems.

"

Such labels as "gifted" or "learning disabled" would have no meaning since they are products of the subject curriculum and adult value systems.

By working together in heterogeneous groups, early adolescents may also have opportunities to experience differing viewpoints on a particular topic. In this way, the themes of the curriculum will take on a more lifelike quality and the concepts of democracy, dignity, and diversity will have an authentic place in the school.

As I write this, the movement for heterogeneous grouping is gaining momentum. The remaining hold-outs seem most often to be parents who believe that their children are more "gifted" than others and thus deserve a differentiated and sometimes separate educational program. Telling our stories and reciting research do not seem to make a difference with these people nor do the admonitions of their own children who would prefer not to be differentially identified from their peers. But as the arguments and statistics fly all around us, we need to remember what Cloyd Hastings (1992, p. 32) wrote: "We need not justify this (heterogeneous grouping) with research, for it is a statement of principle, not of science." My mother, a former teacher and now eighty-six years old, was recently telling me about her own teaching in a heterogeneous classroom, an arrangement she claims benefited all her students. When I asked her what the advantage was for those who were academically highly-able she said this: "They learned to lend a helping hand." Great theories of moral obligation are almost always elegant in their frank simplicity.

Scheduling

I have proposed that a curriculum based on the themes that emerge from the intersection of early adolescent and larger social concerns become the curriculum for the middle school. In doing so I mean that it should be very nearly the whole curriculum and, therefore, that it should take up virtually all of the time in the school day and year. Aside from work within thematic units, some time will be needed for early adolescents to participate in school governance and engage in intramural and other club activities. But, again, this proposal is not meant to take up two or three periods with others devoted to study in separate subject or "exploratory" courses.

Assuming that groups of early adolescents will be assigned to work on particular themes with one or more teachers, the schedule itself ought to be determined by those teachers and students. These people would thus have responsibility for determining how to schedule large group, small group, and individual activities both inside and outside the school. Furthermore, in collaboration with others they would need to determine how long a particular unit would take, whether more than one unit could be taken on simultaneously by a particular group, and so on.

As a result of such scheduling a particular unit may last for any length of time and a series of units may be tied to an overall theme undertaken in the course of a year. Broad themes of the latter type may serve the whole school for a year or different groups may take on different themes each year. In either case it is possible that groups may be formed on a same age or multi-aged basis. Clearly, the limits on such possibilities are only a matter of how imaginative and flexible the people in the school are willing to be.

Beyond those considerations, though, it is in the everyday schedule of learning activities that we will see the new curriculum come to life and, perhaps, understand more fully what it is about. One way of seeing how the "multi-disciplinary" approach presents only limited curriculum progress is to think in terms of the students' schedules. Yes, there may be a central theme to a unit, but the experience of the young people is still essentially a subject-centered one; that is, they still experience the planned curriculum by proceeding from one subject classroom or time slot to another as teachers more or less remind them of the central theme. The "less" part of this is sometimes so covert that some young people are not even aware that they are participating in a multi-disciplinary unit.

" "

The everyday schedule is formed around the activities, problems, or projects that young people are involved with.

In the curriculum I have proposed, content and skill are organically integrated to the extent that identifying subject lines is not only irrelevant, but practically impossible. In this case the everyday schedule is formed around the activities, problems, or projects that young people are involved with. Rather than proceeding from one subject to another, they move from one "integrated" activity to another with the obvious (and serious) possibility that they may stay with one activity until it is fully completed rather than carrying on two or more simultaneously. This, of course, is partly determined by the breadth or scope of the activity.

A word of caution is called for here. In working with integrative curriculum projects young people have sometimes expressed a sense of confusion and ambiguity — what they sometimes call a "lack of structure." I can understand this given that their past school experiences have been defined in terms of specified minutes and clear subject lines. Some teachers have reacted by reinstituting such structures, at times to the relief of young people, since they are something familiar to hang onto. However, I see this as a failure of nerve, of sorts, as it begins to take us right back to where we do not want to be.

The question here should be, "How can we create a sense of structure and familiarity with a new curriculum without corrupting its purpose?" This is an important question in any place where such curriculum reform is undertaken and the response will vary from place to place. One answer, though, may be as simple as some teachers and young people have found. That is, in planning together, a schedule can be made that portrays activities and projects on a daily and weekly basis so that all can anticipate what lies ahead, when projects are to be completed, and so on. As is the key elsewhere, the idea here is to take up the question of structure as a whole group or within a unit steering committee. If we simply revert to old structures and the curriculum that produced them, we ought to ask who the adjustment is really for, the adults or the young people?

Evaluating and reporting student work

Many teachers who have tried to move away from the academic, subject-centered curriculum have eventually found themselves in the very frustrating situation of having to translate their work into the terms of the typical report card. Not only are these ordinarily based upon separate subjects, but they also imply some sort of narrow, quantitative assessment of student work. Thus if the curriculum is going to change, then so will the usual way of assessing and reporting the schoolwork of early adolescents.

—————————— **"** ——————————

If the curriculum is to change, then so will the usual way of assessing and reporting the schoolwork of early adolescents.

In looking at student work in a new curriculum we will have to concern ourselves with a wide variety of possible effects. For example, we will want to know what early adolescents have learned about, how they went about their learning, whether they were able to find personal and social meanings, what activities they engaged in, what projects they undertook, how they portrayed their work, whether they had changed in their attitudes or behaviors during the unit, what resources they used, and so on. For these kinds of effects there are no standardized tests, no norm-referenced standards, and no quantifiable indices. Moreover, letter grades seem almost insulting; that is, how can the work and learning involved be reasonably portrayed in a single letter grade?

In this new curriculum, then, we will have to invent new ways of looking at student work. For example, teachers would likely want to keep careful notes on what is happening with groups and individuals as well as careful records of activities and resources used. Early adolescents would need to keep logs or journals about their work as well as portfolios containing everything that they produced (Rief, 1990). In the end the report of individual and group work would be of a descriptive nature telling what was done, how it was done, and what appear to be the outcomes. Moreover, the development of such descriptions would need to be done through collaboration between students and their teachers as part of the continuous involvement of young people in planning and decision making. This should include, among other things, student involvement in decisions about what is being assessed as well as how it is being assessed and reported. Finally, all records of student experiences, including personal files and report cards, ought to include evaluative notations and descriptions by young people.

―――――――――   ❝❝   ―――――――――

We look for activities that clearly involve the integration of knowledge and skill from a broad range of sources – what we often call "big bang" projects.

While all of that makes sense, it is also the case that breaking out of old categories is a hard thing to do. When we try to create new possibilities, especially when still surrounded by the old structures, there is always the risk (sometimes the temptation) of backsliding. In the present case, report card time is certainly such a moment. Those of us who have worked with an integrative curriculum have found that such moments are less difficult if we are particularly careful about the kinds of activities that we plan with young people. Specifically, we look for activities that clearly involve the integration of knowledge and skill from a broad range of sources — what we often call "big bang" projects.

When our attention is fully focused on these, it is much easier in the end to remember what we were trying to do and to avoid slipping into simply reporting sub-skill or content acquisition. In short, since evaluation is of what we have done, the "doing" itself is where the issue of consistency is resolved.

As this contentious aspect of the curriculum evolves, we will want to remember that it replaces a system of quantitative, short-form assessment that is best known for its inadequacies. Almost everyone can recite "horror" stories of report card experiences for themselves and their children. We know, for example, that grades are generally not motivating for early adolescents, except perhaps for the very few who consistently receive very high grades. As for parent demands that the traditional system be continued, Lounsbury and Vars (1978), for example, report that only ten percent of parents in one district asked for letter grades when given the opportunity to have a more descriptive report.

In the end, though, we ought to heed the research of Mary Strubbe (1989) who reports that, "failing one or more subjects" ranks as a stressful item among early adolescents, on a par with "death of a close friend," "death of a grandparent," and "death of a parent." Looking at these data, one could reasonably suggest that the typical method of assessing and reporting student work is so out of perspective that it ought to be changed whether we get a new curriculum or not.

The middle school in the overall school program

One of the most difficult issues in the middle school movement has been the matter of articulating the program at that level with the elementary and high school programs. In some cases no real effort in this area has been made and since the middle school curriculum has been largely untouched, no substantial problems have arisen. In other cases, where the curriculum has been changed to some degree, middle schools have felt the sting of criticism from the high school.

Insofar as the present curriculum proposal is concerned, the articulation issue may be looked at in at least two different ways. The first is to assume that not much will change in either the elementary or high schools. In that case, the traditional perception that the middle level serves as a break from the elementary curriculum acts in favor of a new curriculum. In other words, whatever that curriculum is, the fact that it is different from the elementary school version makes little difference. At the other end of the middle school, a good deal of work would need to be done to explain the new curriculum to high school educators so that they may rethink their expectations of students and their backgrounds. While they may complain about this, those at the middle level might properly assume that their work has always been criticized and will probably continue to be.

A second way to consider the place of the middle school in the overall school program would be to imagine that the notion of general education would be reconsidered in elementary and high schools as well. For example, it is only in the relatively recent past that elementary schools have moved away from unit teaching around broad themes and toward highly differentiated skill programs and, ironically, departmentalized curriculum forms. On the other hand, proposals for a problems and needs centered version of general education as part of the high school curriculum have been made for years (Lurry and Alberty, 1957; Alberty and Alberty, 1962; Beane, 1980; Jenkins and Tanner, 1992).

While the present curriculum proposal is made in terms of middle schools, its basic assumptions apply to other levels as well. Taken broadly in this way, we might envision its view of general education making up a child-centered version of the entire elementary curriculum and an adolescent-centered version for a part of the high school program, particularly as adolescents begin to make more specific specialization plans for themselves (see Figure 5.1). While these possibilities may seem far-fetched, we can presently look for illustration to some versions of the whole language approach at the elementary level, the growing trend of high schools looking to the middle level for ideas, and such examples as the widely publicized Central Park East School in New York City at the high school level.

Figure 5.1
General Education Across Formal Schooling

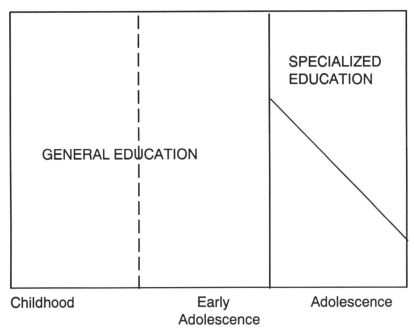

Childhood   Early   Adolescence
                        Adolescence

Teacher education and certification

Proposals for curriculum change almost inevitably include suggestions for changing teacher education. This makes some sense, of course, since teacher education is at least partially based on the academic, subject-centered curriculum and a new curriculum form would presumably call for some change in teacher education. On the other hand, waiting for teacher education to change before undertaking change in the middle school curriculum would most likely mean that we would grow old just talking.

Experience with interdisciplinary instruction should by now have taught us that much more can be initially accomplished by empowering teachers to create curriculum changes and simultaneously learn together how to implement them through inservice education programs and curriculum development projects. At the same time, recent opportunities to develop special certification regulations for middle school teaching offer possibilities for rethinking the roles of teachers at that level while also entering the realm of pre-service teacher education by a "side-door."

In pursuing these possibilities, we will also need to imagine what kind of teachers we might need for a new curriculum. The answer is not simply dual- or multi-certified teachers who can legally offer multi-subject courses (the lack of which partially accounted for the emergence of interdisciplinary teams instead of the revival of single-teacher, block-time core programs).

To implement the middle school curriculum, we will need teachers who are:

- thoroughly knowledgeable about the characteristics of early adolescents and able to make curriculum decisions which reflect this knowledge,

- capable of engaging young adolescents in collaborative, continuing identification of curriculum themes at the local level,

- willing and able to engage in curriculum development projects which create and refine available resources for use in studying identified themes,

- knowledgeable about social issues from many perspectives and willing to develop even greater understanding in this regard,

- willing and able to plan cooperatively with other teachers, early adolescents, and people in the community,

- flexible, imaginative, and tolerant of ambiguity,

- not just subject teachers, but participants in a much broader educational mission with early adolescents.

Research possibilities

Rethinking the middle school curriculum cannot be a careless adventure. We must care about what happens. For this reason, we will need to pay particular attention to the need for research within and around our efforts. Vars (1992) has compiled a bibliography of studies, dating back to the 1930s that investigate aspects of curriculum arrangements beyond the separate subject approach. Among these are many that sought to compare student outcomes from separate subject and non-subject approaches like interdisciplinary, unified studies, and core programs. Such studies are of continuing importance and clearly there is a need to carry them out on a long-term basis, following middle school students through high school and beyond.

However, we also need to turn our attention to the qualitative aspects of curriculum work. For example, what are the experiences of teachers and early adolescents as they plan and carry out integrated curriculum projects? What does it feel like for them? What do the projects look like? How can parents find a place or feel a stake in an integrated curriculum? How does an integrated curriculum interact with institutional features like grouping and scheduling in real schools?

What I am calling for here is not a rejection of quantitative studies, but rather a complimentary body of curriculum stories that can tell us what happens behind, within, and around our curriculum work — more than numbers alone can tell us. If research is to inform our action, then it must be action research that presents the full picture of what happens in a particular place. This notion is, of course, in keeping with the parallel structure where curriculum action is diverse across local places. Moreover, such research may serve to inspire those who decide to take action but are unsure of possibilities and paralyzed by perceived obstacles.

If needed research is about particular places, then it must also be carried out in those places with full participation by the very people who are engaged in curriculum action. I mean here that we need research that is done by teachers and young people and parents who are actually doing the curriculum. We must imagine these people researching such questions as these: What questions and concerns have been raised by early adolescents? What kinds of themes seem to consistently grow out of these questions? Are there any patterns in the kinds of activities that follow from particular questions? What knowledge and skill emerge in an integrated curriculum? What kind of assessment makes sense? What kinds of things do parents want reported and how can they be reported?

These are real and important questions. And they are similar in that all emerge from real curriculum work. We need to know what happens when people try to answer them as well as what kinds of answers they come up with. Here, then, is the kind of research we need, the kind that can take us further in our struggle to continue conversations about the curriculum question.

Summary

Proposals to change the curriculum are often distracted by immediate questions about their implementation. Important as these questions may be, there is a larger need to "talk" about curriculum itself and come to a reasonable consensus about its form and substance. At the same time, we must be aware that when questions of implementation do arise, they may have to be answered outside of current and familiar practices and structures.

The curriculum proposal I have made is a case in point. A first priority must be a wide discourse about early adolescents, the social scene, and the intersection of those two so that its basis might be more fully understood. Such a discourse ought to involve broad participation both inside and outside middle schools by professional educators, parents, other community members, adolescents themselves. Only in this way can authentic curriculum reform receive the commitment that is necessary to sustain it.

By way of illustrative practical arrangements, several seem reasonable to expect. To implement this proposal, middle school educators would need to rethink configurations of teachers, teaching processes, and evaluation procedures. Moreover, the proposal suggests the need for heterogeneous grouping, well-supported curriculum development projects, and changes in teacher education and certification, and appropriate research.

That these kinds of changes may seem overwhelming is not surprising. After all, they emerge from a quite different conception of the curriculum than the one most of us have known and which has almost paralyzed talk about alternative forms. Nevertheless, the history of the middle school movement suggests that almost anything can be accomplished if middle school educators want it badly enough.

Epilogue

A Challenge to the Middle School Movement

Several months before undertaking the first edition of this volume I attended a workshop for middle level educators from over one hundred schools. The schools they represented ranged from some that still reflected a "junior" version of the high school to a few that had been involved in middle level "reform" for over two decades. The former were hard at work trying to develop a better understanding of early adolescence and to find out what more experienced "middle schools" were doing. The talk in these groups centered mainly on institutional features of their school — staffing, scheduling, grouping, and so on — and how those stood in relation to the characteristics of the "kids." Meanwhile, in visiting with those from long-standing, innovative "middle schools," I was struck by their unsettled sense that while they had done a great deal by way of organizational work, there was still something missing. The questions they asked were, "what's next?" and "where do we go from here?"

As we talked over several days it became increasingly clear that in these schools they had asked almost every possible question except, "what about the curriculum?" It is certainly strange to imagine that even these experienced educators who had deliberately experimented with and recreated so many aspects of their schools had missed this most central question. As they began to talk about the curriculum it was apparent that they did not even have a commonly understood language for communicating their thoughts and feelings. While they were in agreement that their reform work was incomplete, signs of conflict and discomfort emerged soon after the curriculum talk began. Yet even in the midst of discomfort they agreed that this was the topic they ought to be discussing.

From this real vignette we may learn some very important things. One is that as more and more middle school educators work out the organizational reform of their schools, if they continue to think about early adolescents and the middle school, they will eventually come to see that organizational "restructuring" is an incomplete version of reform. Another is that theory and practice in the middle school movement have relatively little to offer by way of suggestions about genuine curriculum reform. A third is that no matter how willing people have been to undertake organizational reform, talk and action regarding curriculum change will not come easily. Finally, in anticipation that recognition of the "curriculum hole" will eventually come to others who undertake middle level reform, it would make sense that middle school talk identify this as one of the topics that ought to be considered from the very start. Short of this, continued talk about middle level reform will be incomplete and artificial.

In this volume I have argued a case for thinking in a new way about the middle school curriculum. The case rests on the following line of reasoning:

1. Middle schools ought to be formed around the concept of general and "common," rather than specialized, education.

2. The meaning of general education in the middle school ought to be based upon the widely shared concerns of early adolescents and issues they do and will face in the larger world regardless of what individual paths their lives may follow. In this way the middle school may be both developmentally appropriate and responsive to the concerns of society.

3. Given this meaning, it is apparent that the academic-centered, separate subject approach is not an appropriate way of conceptualizing the middle school curriculum. Moreover, it has other features that call it into question: its historical relations with cultural and intellectual

elites, its roots in questionable learning theory, its myopic view of what makes for a "good life," its tenuous claims about effective learning outcomes, and its narrow view of how people generally use subject matter in their real lives.

4. A more appropriate curriculum for the middle school, rooted in a defensible version of general education, would derive its central themes from the intersection of early adolescent concerns and compelling issues in the larger world.

5. Organizing the curriculum in this way would reposition important subject matter from various subject areas rather than eliminate or ignore it, would open the way for including subject matter historically marginalized by the usual subject approach, and would promote development and application of a wide array of skills.

6. Organizing the curriculum in this way would provide greater opportunities to bring such concepts as democracy, human dignity, and cultural diversity to life in the middle school.

7. Organizing the curriculum in this way would help to make the middle school movement a comprehensive, coherent, and complete version of middle level reform assuming, of course, that this is the actual intention of middle level reformers. And, if that is the intention, such a curriculum would become the whole, planned curriculum of the middle school.

This last point is particularly important. It is hard to imagine that any movement to improve schooling would not take up the curriculum question. Yet it is not at all clear that the middle school movement has had that question on its agenda except in the minds of a handful of "theorists" and some teachers in local schools. Could it be that the curriculum was never really seen as a topic for rethinking? Or, more likely, is it that most middle level "reformers" did not see or fully understand the logical implications of their own reform talk?

The question now is whether those involved in middle school improvement are ready and willing to confront this most central of issues in their work. John Dewey (1938, p. 49) put this issue in a pointed way:

> What avail is it to win prescribed amounts of
> information about geography and history, to win
> ability to read and write, if in the process the indi-
> vidual loses his [or her] own soul: loses his [or her]
> appreciation of things worthwhile, of the values to
> which these things are relative; if he [or she] loses
> desire to apply what he [or she] has learned and, above
> all, loses the ability to extract meaning from his [or
> her] future experiences as they occur.

In the end, perhaps the most compelling way to put the case is to
return to the rhetoric of the middle school movement; that is, to think
in terms of what is good and right for early adolescents. Over the past
three decades we have come to learn more about this group than ever
before. Among our learnings is that personal and social themes are
ascendant in early adolescence. They largely constitute the preoccupy-
ing concerns of early adolescents. At the same time, we would have to
be blind not to notice the many issues that face us in our world and that
do and will impinge upon the lives of early adolescents just as they do
our own.

Taken together (or even separately) these two factors ought to tell
us something about what the curriculum of the middle school ought to
be. Surely there ought to be a way to help early adolescents be very good
early adolescents — to deal with the emerging issues in their lives — and
at the same time to bring them more fully into connection with the real
world in which they live. Surely there must be a way for middle schools
to offer early adolescents something more deeply human than they do
now, more relevant, more compelling, more truly educative. In this
sense, there is a deeper value expression that lies behind the curriculum
proposal I have made. It is to open the hearts and minds of young people
to the possibilities for a more just and humane world — a world in which
human dignity, the democratic way of life, and the prizing of diversity
are more widely shared and experienced. In doing this, we would surely
find our work more complete, more coherent, and more satisfying.

At the same time, however, we must always remember that authentic curriculum reform does not come easily. In doing research for this
work I was struck by how far the middle schools had come in adjusting
organizational features to the characteristics of early adolescents. Yet

I also wondered just how much change the dominant, academic culture of schooling would tolerate. Difficult as the road may have seemed to the present point, advocates of the middle school have not yet had to take a truly contentious stand. My feeling in the end is that the curriculum is just such a place and perhaps the most meaningful one. After all, it is the curriculum, rather than grade level reorganization or teaming, that defines the value of schools for early adolescents — the curriculum that has yet to be on the agenda for "reform." I wonder if we would have gotten so far if it had been part of initial efforts to change middle level schools or, perhaps, if it would have meant the "end game" for the movement just as it may now.

But there is no avoiding the curriculum question. As I write this, the educational spotlight in many places is turned on the middle school. And, many who claim interest in "restructuring" schools are reaching out and grabbing in the middle school movement, appropriating successful organizational changes for the agenda of academic "excellence." This move is made all the easier by our failure to articulate a truly genuine middle school curriculum. As the spotlight is on the middle level, now is not the time to remain silent. Instead, now is the time to take on the middle school curriculum, to put our efforts squarely where our rhetoric has been.

References

Aiken, Wilford. (1941). *The story of the eight year study.* New York: Harper & Row.

Alberty, Harold B., and Alberty, Elsie J. (1962). *Reorganizing the high school curriculum* (rev. ed.). New York: Macmillan.

Alexander, William M. (1962). What educational plan for the in-betweenager? *The NEA Journal 55* (March), 30-32.

Alexander, William M.; Williams, Emmett L.; Compton, Mary; and Prescott, Dan. (1968). *The emergent middle school.* New York: Holt, Rinehart & Winston.

Alexander, William M., and George, Paul S. (1981). *The exemplary middle school.* New York: Holt, Rinehart & Winston.

Apple, Michael W. (1979). *Ideology and curriculum.* London, Boston, and Henley: Routledge and Kegan Paul.

Apple, Michael W. (1982). *Education and power.* Boston and London: Routledge and Kegan Paul.

Apple, Michael W. (1986). *Teachers and texts: A political economy of class and gender relations in education.* New York and London: Routledge and Kegan Paul.

Arnold, John. (1980). Needed: a realistic perception of the early adolescent learner. *Clearinghouse 54* (Winter), 4.

Arnold, John. (1985). A responsive curriculum for early adolescents. *Middle School Journal 16* (May), 3, 14-18.

Beane, James A. (1972). Teacher-student planning: Some practical aspects. *Dissemination Services on the Middle Grades 3,* 1-6.

Beane, James A. (1975). The case for core in the middle school. *Middle School Journal. 6* (Summer), 33-34.

Beane, James A. (1976). Options for interdisciplinary teams. *Dissemination Services on the Middle Grades 7,* 1-6.

Beane, James A. (1980). The general education we need. *Educational Leadership 37* (January), 307-8.

Beane, James A., and Lipka, Richard P. (1986). *Self-concept, self-esteem, and the curriculum.* New York: Teachers College Press.

Beane, James A., Toepfer, Conrad F., Jr., & Allesi, Samuel, Jr. (1986). *Curriculum planning and development.* Boston: Allyn & Bacon.

Beane, James A., and Lipka, Richard P. (1987). *When the kids come first: Enhancing self-esteem.* Columbus, OH: National Middle School Association.

Beane, James A. (1990). *Affect in the curriculum: Toward democracy, dignity, and diversity.* New York: Teachers College Press.

Beane, James A. (1991). The middle school: Natural home of integrated curriculum. *Educational Leadership 49* , 9-13.

Beane, James A. (1992). Turning the floor over: Reflections on *A middle school curriculum. Middle School Journal 23,* 34-40.

Becker, Henry Jay. (1990). Curriculum and instruction in middle grades schools. *Phi Delta Kappan 71* (February), 450-7.

Bloom, Allan D. (1987). *The closing of the American mind.* New York: Simon and Schuster.

Brazee, Chris, and Dibiase, Nick. (1992). We are 7th graders. *The In-between Years 3* (Winter), 7.

Brazee, Edward. (1987). Exploration in the "regular" curriculum. In Edward Brazee (Ed.), *Exploratory curriculum for the middle level.* Rowley, MA: New England League of Middle Schools.

Brazee, Edward. (1989). The tip of the iceberg or the edge of the glacier: Curriculum development in middle schools. *Mainely Middle 1* (Spring), 18-22.

Brodhagen, Barbara, Weilbacher, Gary, & Beane, James (1992). Living in the future: An experiment with an integrative curriculum. *Dissemination Services on the Middle Grades 23,* 1-7.

Bruner, Jerome S. (1960). *The process of education.* Cambridge, MA: Harvard University Press.

Bruner, Jerome S. (1971). The process of education reconsidered. In Robert R. Leeper (Ed.), *Dare to care/dare to act.* Washington, DC: Association for Supervision and Curriculum Development, pp. 19-30.

Burrows, John. (1978). *The middle school: High road or dead end.* London: Woburn.

Burton, William H. (1952). *The guidance of learning activities.* New York: Appleton-Century-Crofts.

Carnegie Council on Adolescent Development. (1989). *Turning points: Preparing American youth for the 21st century.* New York: Carnegie Corporation.

Compton, Mary F. (1984). Balance in the middle school curriculum. In John H. Lounsbury (Ed.), *Perspectives: Middle school education, 1964 - 1984.* Columbus, OH: National Middle School Association.

Cuban, Larry. (1992). What happens to reforms that last: The case of the junior high school. *American Educational Research Journal 29,* 227-251.

Dewey, John. (1915). *The school and society* (rev. ed.). Chicago: University of Chicago Press.

Dewey, John. (1938). *Experience and education.* Bloomington, IN: Kappa Delta Pi.

Dressel, Paul L. (1958). The meaning and significance of integration. In Nelson B. Henry (Ed.), *The integration of educational experiences.* 57th Yearbook of the National Society for the Study of Education. Chicago: University of Chicago Press.

Educational Policies Commission. (1938). *The purposes of education in American democracy.* Washington, DC: National Education Association.

Eichhorn, Donald H. (1966). *The middle school.* New York: The Center for Applied Research in Education.

Everhart, Robert. (1979). *The in-between years: Student life in a junior high school.* Santa Barbara, CA: Graduate School of Education, University of California.

Faunce, Roland C., and Bossing, Nelson L. (1951). *Developing the core curriculum.* New York: Prentice-Hall.

Faunce, Roland C., and Bossing, Nelson L. (1958). *Developing the core curriculum,* 2nd ed. New York: Prentice-Hall.

George, Paul S. and Oldaker, Lynn L. (1985). *Evidence for the middle school.* Columbus, OH: National Middle School Association.

George, Paul S., Stevenson, Chris, Thomason, Julia, and Beane, James (1992). *The middle school — and beyond.* Alexandria, VA: Association for Supervision and Curriculum Development.

Gilligan, Carol. (1982). *In a different voice: Psychological theory and women's development.* Cambridge, MA: Harvard University Press.

Goddson, Ivor (1993). *School subjects and curriculum change* 3rd Edition. Philadelphia, PA: Falmer.

Gross, Bernard M. (1972). *An analysis of the present and perceived purposes, functions, and characteristics of the middle school.* Unpublished Doctoral Dissertation. Philadelphia, PA: Temple University.

Gruhn, William T. and Douglass, Harl R. (1947). *The modern junior high school* . New York: Ronald .

Hargreaves, Andy. (1986). *Two cultures of schooling: The case of middle schools.* London: Falmer.

Hastings, Cloyd. (1992). Ending ability grouping is a moral imperative. *Educational Leadership 50,* 32.

Hirsch, E.D. (1987). *Cultural literacy: What every American needs to know.* Boston: Houghton Mifflin.

Hock, Louise, and Hill, Thomas. (1960). *The general education class in the secondary school.* New York: Holt-Rinehart.

Hopkins, L. Thomas (1937). *Integration: Its meaning and application.* New York: D. Appleton-Century.

Hopkins, L. Thomas. (1941). *Interaction: The democratic process.* New York: D.C. Heath.

Hopkins, L. Thomas. (1955). *The core program: Integration and interaction.* New York: Board of Education of the City of New York.

Hurd, Paul DeHart. (1992). First in the world by 2000. What does that mean. *Education Week XII,* 28.

Jacobs, Heidi Hayes (Ed.). (1989). *Interdisciplinary curriculum.* Alexandria, VA: Association for Supervision and Curriculum Development.

Jenkins, Daniel (Ed.) (1992). *Restructuring for an interdisciplinary curriculum.* Reston, VA: National Association for Secondary School Principals.

Johnson, Mauritz (Ed.). (1980). Toward adolescence: *The middle school years.* 79th Yearbook of the National Society for the Study of Education, Part I. Chicago: University of Chicago Press.

Kindred, Leslie W.; Wolotkiewicz, Rita J.; Mickelson, John M.; and Copelin, Leonard E. (1981). *The middle school curriculum* (2nd ed.). Boston: Allyn and Bacon.

Kliebard, Herbert M. (1986). *The struggle for the American curriculum: 1893-1958.* Boston and London: Routledge and Kegan Paul.

Kliebard, Herbert M., and Wegner, Greg. (1990). Harold Rugg and the reconstruction of the social studies curriculum: The treatment of the Great War in his textbook series. In Thomas S. Popkewitz (Ed.), *The formation of the school subjects.* New York: Falmer.

Leake, Brenda. (1991). Speech presented at the National Middle School Association Conference on Curriculum, Minneapolis, MN.

Lipsitz, Joan. (1984). *Successful schools for young adolescents.* East Brunswick, NJ: Transaction.

Lounsbury, John H., and Vars, Gordon F. (1978). *A curriculum for the middle school years.* New York: Harper & Row.

Lounsbury, John H.; Marani, Jean; and Compton, Mary. (1980). *The middle school in profile: A day in the seventh grade.* Columbus, OH: National Middle School Association.

Lounsbury. John H. (Ed.). (1984). *Perspectives: Middle school education. 1964-1984.* Columbus, OH: National Middle School Association

Lounsbury, John H., and Johnston, Howard J. (1988). *Life in the three 6th grades.* Reston, VA: National Association of Secondary School Principals.

Lounsbury, John H., and Clark, Donald. (1990). *Inside grade eight: From apathy to excitement.* Reston, VA: National Association of Secondary School Principals.

Lurry, Lucille, and Alberty, Elsie. (1957). *Developing a high school core program.* New York: Macmillan.

Meeth, Richard L. (1978) . Interdisciplinary studies: A matter of definition. *Change 10,* 10.

Middle Level Curriculum Project. (1993). Middle level curriculum: In search of self and social meaning. In Tom Dickinson (Ed.), *Readings in middle school curriculum: A continuing conversation.* Columbus, OH: National Middle School Association.

Middle School Journal 18 (August 1987).

Middle School Journal 21 (September 1989).

Monagha, Jennifer, and Saul, Wendy. (1990). The reader, the scribe, the thinker: A critical look at reading and writing instruction. In Thomas S. Popkewitz (Ed.), *The formation of the school subjects.* New York: Falmer.

Moss, Theodore C. (1969). *Middle school.* New York: Houghton Mifflin.

NASSP Council on Middle Level Education. (1985). *An agenda for excellence at the middle level.* Reston, VA: National Association of Secondary School Principals.

National Commission on Excellence in Education. (1983). *A nation at risk: The imperative for educational reform.* Washington, DC: U.S. Government Printing Office.

Oakes, Jeannie. (1987). *Keeping track: Structuring inequality in schools.* New Haven CT: Yale University Press.

Popkewitz, Thomas S. (Ed.). (1987). *The formation of school subjects: The struggle for creating an American institution.* New York: Falmer.

Ravitch, Diane, and Finn, Chester E . (1987) . *What do our 17 year olds know?* New York: Harper and Row.

Reif, Linda. (1990). Finding the value in evaluation: Self-assessment in a middle school classroom. *Educational leadership 47* (March), 24-9.

Smith, B. Othanel.; Stanley, William O.; and Shores, J. Harlan, (1950). *Fundamentals of curriculum development.* New York: Harcourt, Brace, and World.

Staaland, T. Elaine (Ed.). (1987). *A guide to curriculum in home economics.* Madison, WI: Wisconsin Department of Public Instruction.

Stevenson, Chris. (1986). *Teachers as inquirers: Strategies for learning with and about early adolescents.* Columbus, OH: National Middle School Association.

Stevenson, Chris, and Carr, Judith. (1993). *Integrative studies in the middle grades: Dancing through walls.* New York: Teachers College Press.

Stratemeyer, Florence; Forkner, Hamden L.; McKim, Margaret G.; and Passow, A. Harry. (1947). *Developing a curriculum for modern living.* New York: Teachers College, Columbia University.

Strubbe, Mary. (1989). An assessment of early adolescent stress factors. In David B. Strahan (Ed.), *1989 research annual: Selected studies.* Columbus, OH: National Middle School Association.

Sykes, Charles J. (1988). *Profscam: Professors and the demise of higher education.* Washington, DC: Regnery Gateway.

Tanner, Daniel, and Tanner, Laurel N. (1980). *Curriculum development: theory into practice.* New York: Macmillan.

Tanner, J.M. (1962). *Growth in adolescence.* Oxford: Blackwell Scientific Publications.

Tronto, Joan C. (1987). Beyond gender difference to a theory of care. *Signs: Journal of women in culture and society 12* (Summer), 664-663.

Van Til, William; Vars, Gordon F.; and Lounsbury, John H. (1961). *Modern education for the junior high school years*, Indianapolis, IN: Bobbs-Merrill (second edition, 1967).

Vars, Gordon F. (1966). Can team teaching save the core curriculum? *Phi Delta Kappan 47* (January), 258-262.

Vars, Gordon F. (1987). *Interdisciplinary teaching in the middle grades.* Columbus, OH: National Middle School Association.

Vars, Gordon F. (1992). *A bibliography of research on the effectiveness of block-time, core, and interdisciplinary team teaching programs.* Kent State University, Unpublished.

Wright, Grace S. (1958). *Block-time classes and the core program.* Washington, DC: U.S. Government Printing Office.

Zapf, Rosalind M. (1959). *Democratic processes in the secondary class-room.* Englewood Cliffs, NJ: Prentice-Hall.